MADAME CHOCOLATE'S
B·O·O·K·O·F
Divine Indulgences

ELAINE SHERMAN

Contemporary Books, Inc.
Chicago

For Steven, David, and Jaime
Always reach for the stars!
And for Jerry

Library of Congress Cataloging in Publication Data

Sherman, Elaine.
  Madame Chocolate's book of divine indulgences.

  Includes index.
  1. Cookery (Chocolate)   I. Title
TX767.C5S53   1984   641.6'374   84-17635
ISBN 0-8092-5373-9

Published by Contemporary Books, Inc.
180 North Michigan Avenue, Chicago, Illinois 60601
Manufactured in the United States of America
Library of Congress Catalog Card Number: 84-17635
International Standard Book Number: 0-8092-5373-9

Published simultaneously in Canada by Beaverbooks, Ltd.
195 Allstate Parkway, Valleywood Business Park
Markham, Ontario L3R 4T8 Canada

Contents

Preface

Can you imagine life without chocolate? I can't! My earliest memories of chocolate are of my father, who lined up pieces of chocolate on the arm of his favorite chair—a half pound or more. They were not to be touched by anyone under penalty of death, or even worse. It was my first encounter with a chocoholic, my own father. He was my model, my inspiration. My mother could never become a chocoholic. My father left no piece of candy—except the marzipan. Surprisingly, mother is a marzipan-lover.

My mother had very little interest in cooking and baking. She is the lucky one—first there was my grandmother, and then I came along to share the kitchen. She is always available to sample and her appreciation is a great encouragement to me.

And my grandmother—wonder surrounded her. Grandma Rosie loved to bake and cook. She had a magic touch, the wonderful hands of a good baker. Her doughs were divine, cakes delicious, cookies and brownies superb, and she made her own candy. My mother was an only child and my brother Stanley and I were Grandma Rosie's only grandchildren. Being her only granddaughter I cooked and baked with her. She was a wonderful teacher, and now in her 90s, she still answers my questions and gives her kitchen hints and suggestions.

Our aunts, uncles, cousins and many friends made up a close-knit group. The love and warmth of family and friends with good things to eat made home a happy place. My brother and I followed the example of our parents and opened our home to our young friends. They enjoyed the fun and loved the treats.

Life went on. Grammar school became a memory. High school brought love, and college brought marriage. Suddenly I had an apartment and, best of all, a kitchen of my own. I entertained. I baked. I cooked. I loved it! Special days became a special reason for entertaining family and friends— customs were established that exist to this day. Menus were set down and always, yes always, there was chocolate. I carried on with traditional family recipes—but there was always chocolate.

The best years of my life came. My children were born: first my sons, Steven and David, and then my daughter, Jaime. A new horizon appeared. It was fun to bake cookies and brownies and cupcakes and all kinds of goodies for my children and share their delight. Our house became the meeting place for all of their friends. The kids loved it; it always smelled good. My friends and their children were there, too. I was the cook and baker among my friends. My nephew and nieces were there, too. One wanted brownies, another wanted Auntie Lane's chocolate chip cookies, and another has now graduated to chocolate crêpes.

Suddenly my marriage was over but life wasn't. The fun parts were still ahead. The children were growing to be the kind, gentle, and loving young people they are now. Opportunity came to study cooking with Master Chef John Snowden. He was a wonderful teacher, and I couldn't learn enough. Cooking was my thing! I graduated and was asked to teach cooking for an adult education program. I took advantage of that, too. I loved it! I found my niche. My father passed away, and the arm of his chair is now bare. A new man entered my life, and Jerry would give me encouragement to accomplish much that I have.

The Gourmet Revolution started, and a store was born, a gourmet shop with a cooking school. My children encouraged me and helped me do it. It was one wonderful experience after another. The cooks, the bakers, the authors, the chefs—everyone came. James Beard, Barbara Kafka, Simone Beck, Julie Dannenbaum, Perla Meyers, Maida Heatter, Jacques Pepin, Marcella Hazan, Jean Banchet, Jane Freiman, Marion Cunningham, Abby Mandel, and many others (who may not be mentioned but who are loved and their friendships treasured) passed through the kitchen of The Complete Cook. It was exciting. It was electric! And it was delicious! In the repertoire of recipes, there was always chocolate. Chocolate was sold in the shop, which was among the first to recognize that premium-quality chocolate was coming to the home kitchen. It was a natural. The largest supermarkets could offer only a limited variety of chocolate. Many thousands of pounds were sold. I loved it, I learned, I soaked in as much knowledge as I could and stored it away.

Steven, David, Jaime, and Jerry were part of it, too. The children were getting older, Steven went off to college, David to high school, Jaime was fast approaching her teens, and I would go off to San Francisco each winter, for a week or so, to study with James Beard and Barbara Kafka. They enabled me to refine my palate. I learned to taste, to be discriminating.

An economic squeeze came, and the doors of The Complete Cook closed forever. The memories, however, will never disappear. The friendships will never fade.

A year was required to catch up with myself, to mourn and to grieve. It was time to begin again. The children encouraged it. Jerry was ready to start with me. An idea was conceived. It was nurtured for some time. Friends were helpful, encouragement was there, their minds were available for picking. Then Madame Chocolate, a chocolate mail-order catalog, was born! It was the first of its kind. It was warmly welcomed into the world. It made chocolate available—good chocolate, delicious chocolate—to everyone everywhere. Catalog requests poured in; chocolate was shipped out. The United States found chocolate.

We finally woke up and caught up with the rest of the world. We ate fine chocolate desserts in restaurants, we bought chocolates for previously unheard of prices, we jogged and craved a truffle, we frequented fine bakeries. Suddenly we discovered that our homemade brownies tasted flat. We were using the same chocolate we had always used, but our baked goods didn't taste as good as the wonderful restaurant desserts did. "Why?" we asked. The restaurant chefs and bakers and the chocolatiers had learned that fine chocolate was available in the United States. The person at home couldn't find it. Then came Madame Chocolate. Now you can buy the same chocolate the professionals do. Many kinds of chocolate are now available. Your brownies will be a treat to savor. They will be deep, dark, dense and, oh, so chocolaty and sensual.

This book is a result of what has come before. I always clipped recipes, first for the kids, then for my guests, and some treasured ones came from The Complete Cook. Customers shared them, friends sent them, and I begged for them. I baked them and tasted them; my neighbors ate them. I varied the chocolates, just as you should do. I found that every time you change the chocolate, you change the taste.

I have given you my best, the most delicious of all, my all-time favorites. This is a treasury of my favorite recipes. I did not stand in my kitchen for two years to create them for you. I collected recipes for many years, and these are my absolute favorites. I baked these, changed them when necessary, made them work, and I offer them to you. Food people will tell you that, if you get one good recipe out of a cookbook, you get your money's worth. Well, friends, I bought all those cookbooks for you, I bought the magazines, I subscribed to the newsletters, and I baked and tested. I did it for myself first, and now for you! You will find many recipes to satisfy the chocoholic in you. The best have contributed their best. It's in your hands—you're into chocolate. Don't wash your hands—lick them clean.

Acknowledgments

A special thank you to:

My children, Steven, David, and Jaime, a love-filled thank you for your encouragement in everything I've done. You are my inspiration.

Jerry, for his love, his constant support, his willingness to help, and for his unending patience.

My mother and father, for the love, encouragement, and guidance they gave me from the very first moment.

My brother, for always being there.

My grandmother, for starting it all! You taught me that there's love in the kitchen.

Shash, for her love.

I am most grateful for the support of two very special people whose assistance made this book a reality:

Susie Skoog, for her skillful, excellent recipe testing, for coping with me when I said, "Just test one more, please," for sharing so many of her wonderful recipes, and most of all for her friendship.

Neil Spinner, for his guidance and patience in teaching me how to use the word processor, for his unbelievable calm in response to my cries for help (if it weren't for him I would still be typing), for listening, for caring, and for his expert tasting.

I am also grateful to:

Elaine González, for giving of herself, for all the chocolate roses, for the chocolate advice that is available day and night. I am happy to call you friend.

Jane Freiman, for believing in me and saying, "Do it! I know you can," and for her friendship.

Nancy Crossman, my editor, for believing in the book and for making it happen, fast.

Michael Bortz, for sending the truffles that grace this cover across the United States to be photographed.

Carol DeMasters, for doing so much to help start this collection of recipes.

Jolene Worthington, Richard Klein, and Lynn McEwan who gave this book its style.

My friends, who, throughout the years, have always believed in me—Arline and Bud,

Helene and Lennie, Cookie and Aaron, Mary and Gene, Erika and Girard, Gloria and Shelly, Elaine and Jerry, and Maxine and Tom.

Sandra, who will always be missed!

My chocolate tasters, Lindsay, Anne, Sasha, and Kristin, who were never too full to take another bite.

This book could not have happened without the advice and guidance of the following professional chocolate people:

Malcome Blue, Nestlé; John Buzzard, Wilbur; Lenore Cooney, Dudley-Anderson-Yutzy; Dennis DeDomenico, Ghirardelli; Anne Goldner, Uster; Gary Guittard, Guittard; Gene Kaplan, Amazon de Choix; Richard O'Connell, Chocolate Manufacturer's Association; Ed Opler, Jr., World's Finest Chocolate; Rudi Sprungli, Lindt; Marie-Claude Stockl, Nestlé; Larry Walbrun, Ambrosia; and Frank Walker, Maracorp.

"GOOD LIVING
is an act of intelligence,
by which we choose things
which have an agreeable taste
rather than those which do not."

Brillat-Savarin

Introduction

Americans have come out of the closet. We are chocoholics and we're proud of it!

As a nation that was raised on chocolate which was excessively sweetened and lacking in richness, we have now become better informed and have developed discriminating tastes. Our plebeian palates have become more sophisticated. We travel the world, frequent food specialty shops, shop in epicurean sections of fine department stores, and dine in fine restaurants. By reducing the sugar in our foods and in our chocolate bars, we have developed a greater appreciation of chocolate itself. The nuances and subtleties of taste take on greater significance.

All the above has helped to educate our palates. We are a people that learns and changes for the better. During the Gourmet Revolution of the '70s and early '80s, we learned about mustards, oils, vinegars, and cheeses just to name a few foods. We changed our eating habits. Today we seek out specialty produce and look for a greater variety of special foods. We are now a nation that does not shop only in our neighborhood grocery store. We have been known to drive two hours to find the butcher who does his own slaughtering to make bratwurst. We go across town to a specialty store that carries unusual food items, both fresh and bottled. We spend our vacations seeking out little stores, looking for foods as we once did for antiques. We frequent ethnic restaurants, always on the lookout for new food ideas to try at home. We have special cakes shipped across country to us because "they're good." We no longer just take a trip. We now travel the United States regionally. We long to experience fresh crab in Maryland, gumbo in New Orleans, barbecue in Kansas City, chili in Texas, country ham in Louisville, and the most innovative food of all, California cuisine.

Yes, we are finally catching up with the rest of the world. Europeans are coming here to see what we are all about. We are discriminating, we are innovative, and we are open to new tastes, new ideas, and new foods. We have become a sensual people. We are open to experiences.

Chic is to have dined with Jean Banchet, Alice Waters, Paul Prudhomme, and Wolfgang Puck. It is to your advantage to have studied with James Beard, Barbara Kafka, Perla Meyers, and Maida Heatter (to name a few). Your cooking repertoire should include pasta, gravlax, Szechuan eggplant, enchiladas, and pasticcio. You should have tasted Godiva, Neuhaus, d'Orsay, Michelle Guerard, and Dilletante chocolates. And now, to be really chic, you should be intimately familiar with Callebaut, Lindt, Valrhôna, Ghirardelli, Guittard, Nestlé, Tobler, Wilbur, and Ambrosia.

Americans found gourmet chocolates. Chocolate and its infinite varieties are becoming household words. We are at the threshold of the Chocolate Revolution. We are on to better things. We have a national affliction settling upon us—and we can't get enough.

In 1860 Americans consumed three-quarters of a pound of chocolate per person per year; that was 1,181,054 pounds of chocolate. Today we consume 9.4 pounds per person per year for a total of more than 2 billion pounds per year. Ah, yes, we're getting there, but the nicest part is that we have a long way to go. The Swiss eat 20 pounds per person per year, so join the fun!

We are consumed with chocolate pastries. We read the dessert menu before we order the main course. We bake 7 billion chocolate chip cookies per year. We are proud of our heritage because chocolate chip cookies, brownies, and fudge are strictly American. But we go far beyond the baking basics; we are deeply into chocolate mousse, chocolate ice cream, chocolate soufflés, chocolate puddings, and chocolate cheesecakes. We have learned that the better the ingredients, the better the dessert.

Now Americans are choosing their baking chocolate with the same awareness and attention to the subtle nuances that they apply to their eating chocolate. Only recently have our tastebuds become refined enough to understand Gianduja and Orange Lait. Our minds are now food-refined enough to allow us to substitute these tastes in old recipes. We understand that the better the chocolate, the better the cake. We are looking for new experiences, and finally they are here. Fine chocolates, both domestic and foreign, are available for use in your kitchen. Now your pies will be sumptuous, your cakes celestial, your mousses seductive, and your brownies deep, dark, and dense.

We have come full circle since Ruth Wakefield took a simple butter drop cookie, added chopped-up chocolate, and created the chocolate chip cookie. She called them Toll House cookies after her restaurant. Each cookie had chocolate in it, but the pieces were not even and each cookie contained a different amount of chocolate. Nestlé came along and created semisweet chocolate morsels. Toll House cookies contain even-sized pieces of chocolate in every cookie. Today's cookies are changing again. We are moving back to random-sized chocolate chunks.

Not only are chunks available to the home baker, but so are chocolate chips in great variety. There are milk chocolate, bittersweet, and semisweet chips. Aside from the conventional size chip, there are now mini, maxi, and supermaxi (*Buds*). We use them in, between, and on top of our cookies.

The world of baking is expanding. Now, not only can Johnny bake; but he also has a great choice in the flavor, size, and shape of chocolate he uses.

We've dispelled the myths of chocolate and added the mystery. We know that chocolate is not responsible for acne, that chocolate contains a protein that inhibits bacterial growth on teeth, that chocolate chip cookies are among snack foods that least promote tooth decay, that chocolate is a natural food, and that chocolate contains phenylethylamine, a substance that is produced in the brain of a person in love.

> Chocolate is not only pleasant of taste, but it is also a veritable balm of the mouth, for the maintaining of all glands and humours in a good state of health. Thus it is, that all who drink it, possess a sweet breath.

> Doctor Stephani Blancardi, Amsterdam, 1705

This book is divided according to dessert type. This organization should facilitate your selection of recipe for the purpose required. Cookies, considered snack foods, can be served as desserts. Cakes, which are traditional desserts, may be the focal point of social gatherings when served with beverages ranging from champagne to coffee. Truffles and fudge can complement a sweet buffet or may serve as treats. The host or hostess, today, has great latitude in recipe selection. The same chocolate mousse which culminates an elegant dinner at one time, can be a picnic basket treat for a concert in the park. I urge you to review the whole book and let your chocolate fall where it may.

You may alter the recipes to satisfy a wide range of palates. The availability of a broad variety of chocolate for home baking has brought fresh, vibrant taste to chocolate dessert making. Prepare it the way it is written, at least the first time. Then experiment to suit your special taste. One sweetness of chocolate may be substituted for another. Flavorings and nuts can be changed. Frostings and glazes are interchangeable. Bake your way through this book and then begin to experiment.

This is a unique book. In addition to the recipes and general baking tips, I have included tasting instructions and party ideas. The enjoyment that you and your guests will get from sampling your baking treats will make the next baking experience more delightful.

This collection has been accumulated over many years. The recipes, some old favorites, some created and inspired by well-known cooks and bakers as well as many nonprofessionals have all been enjoyed. I have persuaded these artists to share their recipes.

If you have a favorite chocolate recipe—please share it. Send it to me at Madame Chocolate. I sincerely hope that you will work with these recipes and have as much fun and pleasure in your kitchen as I have had. I know your family, friends, and guests will be as delighted in your home as people have been in my home.

1

Chocolate Past, Chocolate Present

There is little doubt that the Mayans were familiar with cacao earlier than 600 A.D. They established the earliest known cacao plantations in Central America and then brought the trees to South America. As early as the year 1000, cacao beans were used as money and were a valuable commodity.

The history of chocolate is of American origin. When the Pinta, Niña, and Santa Maria set sail from Spain in 1492 for a new route to the spices and riches of the East, the New World as well as chocolate were unimaginable. Columbus brought some of these brown beans to the court of Ferdinand and Isabella, but there was little or no interest in them.

On Good Friday in the year 1519 the Spanish explorer Hernando Cortez appeared off the coast of Mexico. The Mexican emperor, Montezuma, was filled with dread because of the strange-looking, weapon-carrying strangers on his shores. He believed Cortez to be the God of Air, Quetzalcoatl, who had been banished long before. This belief would lead to Montezuma's downfall and present the empire of Mexico to the Spaniards. Montezuma tried to appease this god in the hope that he would disappear, as legend says he had once done. He sent gold, silver, and jewels to Cortez along with cacao beans, which were of great value to the Aztecs, serving as currency and used in the preparation of a drink that the emperor and the upper class considered too good for the common folk. It was called *chocolatl*, and it is believed that Montezuma drank it by the potful. It is said to have enhanced his sexual prowess and that he always had a gobletful before entering his harem. The Aztecs believed chocolate brought them wisdom, understanding, and great energy. It was a very bitter, cold drink and didn't appeal much to Cortez and his men. He made preparations to leave Mexico, but before he did he established cacao plantations in the name of Spain. He also took home the cacao and the knowledge of how to prepare it.

When Cortez returned to Spain the Spaniards didn't care for this "divine" drink because it was so bitter. Eventually they added hot water and sugar to it, with vanilla and cinnamon, and created a beverage treat that would spread to the rest of the world. Ironically, the craze that started in the New World would take more than two centuries to return. The Spaniards kept cacao a secret for almost 100 years before a Spanish princess married Louis XIII and brought the art of drinking chocolate to the French court in 1615. Chocolate houses appeared, where the populace gathered to sip and gossip. This was the predecessor of the present-day coffee klatsch. Chocolate was believed to be delicious and health-giving, but it was a beverage and only for the privileged.

In 1753 the Swedish naturalist Carolus Linnaeus named the chocolate plant *Theobroma cacao*, or "food of the gods, cacao," taking the name from the Greek *theos*, meaning "god," and *broma*, meaning "food."

Chocolate spread to England, Italy, Germany, and Switzerland. In 1755 it came back to America where John Hanan and Dr. James Baker opened a chocolate-processing house in Massachusetts. The company bearing the Baker name is known to us today.

Little changed in the way chocolate was prepared until the nineteenth century. The pods were gathered, fermented, roasted to develop flavors, cracked, and shelled, and the resulting nibs were ground and pressed into cakes which were broken up to make the drink Europe loved.

The Europeans, and the Swiss in particular, did the most to refine chocolate into the form we know today. In 1828 C. J. van Houten produced cocoa, by pressing some of the cocoa butter from the chocolate. He used an alkali to remove acidity and bitterness from the powder. Today this is known as *Dutch process cocoa*. At that point drinking chocolate took on the taste we know today. In 1876 Daniel Peter, true to his Swiss heritage, added milk to chocolate and invented milk chocolate. But Peter needed the help of his compatriot, Henri Nestlé, who perfected the manufacture of condensed milk. In 1879 Rodolphe Lindt added additional cocoa butter to chocolate to produce a smoother chocolate that melts on the tongue. The discoveries of Peter and Lindt were essential to the current manufacture of chocolate.

In the late 1800s American chocolate manufacturers, using the wisdom of their European counterparts, opened across the United States—H. O. Wilbur & Sons in Philadelphia, Ghirardelli and Guittard in northern California.

Each chocolate manufacturer selects his own blend of beans to produce a particular chocolate flavor. The blend of beans is a principal factor in flavor differences among chocolates. Other factors, though of less significance, are the roasting, conching or grinding of the bean, and cocoa butter content. Chocolate manufacturers guard their formulas very carefully.

The bean, which is worshipped by those of us who love chocolate, grows on trees within 20 degrees of the Equator, in the tropical rain forests that enhance its growth. There are cacao plantations in many countries, but the largest producers are the Ivory Coast, Ghana, Algeria, and Brazil. The cacao tree grows only in the hottest regions of the world, bounded by the Tropics of Cancer and Capricorn. The annual yield per tree is 20–30 pods. Each pod contains 25–40 seeds or beans, and it takes 400 beans to produce a pound of chocolate.

There are two principal varieties of cocoa beans: Criollo and Forastero. The Criollo is the finest and is used in the production of high-quality chocolate and for blending. It accounts for 10 percent of the world crop. The remaining 90 percent is harvested from the trees of the Forastero genus. It has a wide range of qualities.

In the production of chocolate the first step is the harvest of the pods. The pods are opened and the seed kernels, with the surrounding white pulp, are scraped out and subjected to fermentation. The fermentation process is most important in the production of high-quality raw chocolate. During the process the pulp-sugar is broken down and the heat produced by fermentation destroys the germination properties of the cocoa beans. The astringent and bitter taste diminishes, and new substances are formed that will eventually produce the cocoa aroma we all recognize. The beans are then dried, bagged, and shipped throughout the world.

The art of chocolate making takes over. The beans are roasted at about 250°F. (and as with coffee and nuts, cocoa beans become more wholesome and acquire an improved aroma when roasted). Depending on the purpose for which the chocolate is intended, the beans are more or less intensely roasted. The roasting process loosens the husk of the bean, leaving the nib. The nibs, blended according to closely guarded recipes of the manufacturers, are crushed and ground. The crushed beans, which are still fairly coarse, are again ground and crushed to a fine paste. The heat generated by this process causes the cocoa butter contained in the nib to melt, producing a thick liquid mixture. During the cooling, this mixture sets and is called *chocolate liquor*. We also know it as unsweetened, bitter, or baking chocolate. The chocolate liquor is treated in different ways, depending on the desired finished product. If the cocoa butter is pressed out, cocoa is obtained. If additional cocoa butter is added with sugar, eating chocolate is produced. The amount of added sugar will determine the type: bittersweet (the least sweet and most chocolaty-tasting), semisweet, or sweet (the most sugar added). If milk solids are added, milk chocolate is produced.

The mixture travels through a conching machine. Conching is a flavor development process, during which the bitter taste gradually disappears and the flavor is fully produced. It is a kneading action, with heavy rollers that move the chocolate back and forth for a few hours to a few days. The greater the time in the conching machine, the finer the finished chocolate.

After conching, the chocolate undergoes a tempering process and is shaped into bars of varying sizes. Most are the 10-pound bars that are produced for the baking and confectionery industry.

Chocolate reaches us in many ways: as cocoa and as chocolate bars, as coating for filled candies, as a part of the filling in candies, and in chips, bars, and pieces for use in making these recipes.

2

Chocolate Facts and Fantasies

Chocolate brings to mind marvelous gratification:
    Children . . . relish it.
    Lovers . . . share it.
    Chocoholics . . . stash it.
    Stockbrokers . . . dabble in it.
    Wealthy people . . . lavish in it.
    Pregnant women . . . crave it.
    Designers . . . market it.
    Women . . . need it.
    Sensualists . . . indulge in it.
    Pagans . . . worship it.
    Hedonists . . . enjoy it.
    Everyone . . . eats it!

Chocolate is heavenly, mellow, sensual, deep, dark, sumptuous, gratifying, potent, dense, creamy, seductive, suggestive, rich, excessive, silky, smooth, luxurious, celestial.

Chocolate is downfall, happiness, pleasure, love, ecstasy, fantasy.

Chocolate can be melted, formed, shaped, curled, grated, drizzled, molded, scraped, coated, frozen, baked, dipped, sprinkled, sculpted.

Chocolate makes us wicked, guilty, sinful, healthy, chic, happy.

More than 240 million chocolate morsels are purchased in the United States every day.

Americans bake more than 7 billion chocolate chip cookies per year.

The methodology of making chocolate hasn't changed since the turn of the century.

Chocolate contains: Vitamin A, Phosphorus, Potassium, Calcium, Riboflavin, Iron, Niacin, and Thiamine.

Chocolate contains phenylethylamine, a chemical produced by human beings when in love.

Chocolate causes certain endocrine glands to secrete hormones that affect your feelings and behavior by making you happy. Therefore, it counteracts depression, in turn reducing the stress of depression. Your stress-free life helps you maintain a youthful disposition, both physically and mentally. So, eat lots of chocolate!

"Chocolate makes otherwise normal people melt into strange states of ecstasy."—John West, Botany 20 Class (first U.S. college-level chocolate class), Berkeley, California.

Chocolate is America's favorite flavor.

Quality chocolate means chocolate with no preservatives—highly refined chocolate with extra cocoa butter, conched for days, and ultrasmooth.

The smell of chocolate has been magic since the time of the Mayans.

Approximately 90 percent of all chocolate consumed in the United States is milk chocolate.

The Russians call it *shokoladno;* the Italians, *cioccolate;* the Germans *schokolade;* the French, *chocolat;* the Spanish, *chocolate.*

Chocolate is a national affliction—we can't get enough of it!

Americans eat 9.4 pounds of chocolate per person per year, while the Swiss eat 20 pounds per year. Let's catch up!

"IT HAS BEEN shown as proof positive that carefully prepared chocolate is as healthful a food as it is pleasant; that it is nourishing and easily digested . . . [and] that it is above all helpful to people who must do a great deal of mental work."

Brillat-Savarin

3

Types
of
Chocolate:
Tastes and
Textures

Americans are in the throes of a Chocolate Revolution. The demand for quality chocolate for baking and candy-making is growing as people discover the sensuous goodness of fine chocolate. The chocolates listed below have been judged by me, Madame Chocolate, to be the finest in the world. They are professional-quality chocolates once available only to the baking and confectionery industry. They are available in sizes from 7 ounces to 5 kilos (11 pounds), depending on the manufacturer. The recipes in *Madame Chocolate's Book of Divine Indulgences* were tested with chocolates listed below.

Unsweetened: Known as *baking, cooking,* or *bitter chocolate* and intended for all kinds of baking

World's Finest
Valrhôna Extra Cocoa Pâté
Wilbur Gourmet Baking Bar
Callebaut Unsweetened

Bittersweet: Slightly sweetened dark chocolate used for desserts, baking, and candy-making; interchangeable with semisweet; will give the most intense chocolate taste

Poulain Bittersweet
Valrhôna Extra Bitter
Lindt Courante Especiale
Ghirardelli Bittersweet
Callebaut Bittersweet

Semisweet: Sometimes called *sweet chocolate*; the French chef's choice for baking; an all-purpose chocolate that can be interchanged with bittersweet, if desired

Carma Bourbon Vanilla
Lindt Excellence
Guittard French Vanilla
Ghirardelli Queen
Nestlé "Peter" Burgundy
Nestlé "Peter" Swiss Heritage Chocolat D'Or
Callebaut Semi Sweet

Milk: America's favorite chocolate; best for pies, sauces, puddings, and candy-making

Carma Des Alpes

Lindt "Au Lait"
Guittard Old Dutch
Ghirardelli Bay Bridge
Nestlé "Peter" Broc
Nestlé "Peter" Swiss Heritage Alpine
Callebaut Milk

White Chocolate: Made of cocoa butter, sugar, and milk solids; used for mousses, frostings, sauces, cakes, and candy-making

Carma Ivory
Lindt Blancor
Nestlé Snow Cap
Callebaut White

Sweet Harmony: A sophisticated mélange of flavors, such as a combination of hazelnut and milk chocolate or orange and milk chocolate; used for mousses, sauces, cheesecakes, and bombes

Lindt Gianduja
Callebaut Gianduja
Valrhôna Orange Lait

When you use better-quality chocolate you enhance the taste of your finished dessert or candy.

Chocology: Definitions of Chocolate Terms

BITTERSWEET CHOCOLATE: A product made from chocolate liquor by adding cocoa butter and a small amount of sugar to it. The most intensely flavored chocolate.

BLOOM: A whitish cast appearing on chocolate when exposed to varying temperature changes. It does not affect the chocolate's quality.

CACAO BEANS: The fruit of the cacao tree. The source of chocolate.

CHOCOLATE LIQUOR: The material obtained from grinding, liquefying, and pan cooling the chocolate nibs. It is available as unsweetened, bitter, or baking chocolate. It is edible but not palatable.

COCOA BUTTER: The vegetable fat component of chocolate. It is pressed from the chocolate liquor in the production of cocoa. It is added to the liquor in the production of chocolate.

COCOA POWDER: A product obtained by removing some of the cocoa butter from the chocolate liquor under pressure. Low-fat cocoa contains less than 10 percent cocoa butter. Breakfast cocoa must contain a minimum cocoa butter content of 22 percent.

CONFECTIONERY COATING: Artificial chocolate. A flavored vegetable fat (other than cocoa butter) product. The chocolate-flavored coatings contain cocoa.

CONCHING: A grinding process in which the chocolate is put through a kneading action. During this process volatile constituents are driven off, producing a desired flavor in the chocolate. The chocolate is free from harshness and is very smooth.

COUVERTURE: Chocolate with additional cocoa butter, giving it a beautiful patina and shiny finish.

DUTCH PROCESS: A process in the production of cocoa in which an alkali is used, neutralizing the acid, removing bitter taste, and imparting a darker color.

MILK CHOCOLATE: A chocolate product produced from chocolate liquor, cocoa butter, sugar, milk powder, and flavorings. America's favorite chocolate.

NIBS: The edible portion of the cocoa bean. Cacao beans are roasted, outer shell removed, to reveal the meat, or nib. A nib contains 50 percent cocoa butter.

SEIZING: The tightening of chocolate that occurs if a drop or two of water splashes it by mistake. It can be remedied with the addition of vegetable shortening or cocoa butter added a teaspoon at a time.

SEMISWEET CHOCOLATE: A chocolate product produced from chocolate liquor, cocoa butter, sugar, and flavoring (generally vanilla or vanillin).

SWEET CHOCOLATE: *See* semisweet chocolate.

TEMPERING: A process that consists of heating and cooling the chocolate through continuous mixing to ensure the development of stable cocoa butter crystals distributed evenly throughout the mass of chocolate. The tempered chocolate has good texture and uniform glossy color.

THEOBROMA CACAO: The tree upon which cacao pods grow in dense tropical rain forests.

WHITE CHOCOLATE: Cocoa butter, sugar, and milk powder. Contains no chocolate liquor, so it is not considered "real" chocolate in the United States.

VISCOSITY: The fluidity of chocolate.

4

The Art of Working with Chocolate

How to Sample Chocolate

1. Look at it: it should be dark, shiny, and smooth.
2. Smell it: it should have a wonderful aroma.
3. Break it: it should break clean.
4. Taste it: it should have a full-mouth taste with no unpleasant aftertaste. The taste will stay on your tongue long after the chocolate is swallowed.
5. Melt it: it should melt smooth and not grainy.

How to Melt Chocolate

Double Boiler

Chop chocolate into small pieces and place in the top part of a double boiler over hot, not boiling, water. Stir until chocolate is melted and smooth and remove from the heat.

Heavy Saucepan

Chop chocolate into small pieces and place in a heavy-bottomed saucepan. Use this method when combining chocolate with other ingredients such as butter or 2 tablespoons or more of liquid.

Oven Melting

Chop chocolate into small pieces. Preheat oven to 300°F. *Turn oven off.* Place chocolate in a bowl, place in oven, and let stand until melted. Use a chocolate thermometer to be sure chocolate does not go above 120°F.

Microwave

Chop chocolate into small pieces. Place in a microwave-safe vessel and microwave on high for 30 seconds. Chocolate retains its shape in the microwave, so remove and stir. Microwave on high for additional 30-second periods, stirring after each 30-second period until chocolate is melted.

Problems with melting come from too much heat, no matter which method you use to melt it. Chocolate will stiffen and burn. Caution is advised! You must learn to respect chocolate and follow directions exactly.

How to Temper Chocolate

Melting Procedure

1. Hold the bulb end of a chocolate thermometer (80 to 120-degree range) under running tap water until it registers exactly 120°F., or heat the water on the stove to achieve that temperature. Fill the bottom of a double boiler with enough 120-degree water to touch the bottom and sides of the top vessel, adjusting the water level, if necessary, so that it does not float. Maintain this temperature reading throughout the melting procedure.

2. Fill the top vessel with a portion of chopped chocolate. (Guard against splashing water into it!) After about five minutes, begin to stir the mixture. As it melts, add more and more of the remaining chocolate, stirring it frequently to assure a uniformity of temperature throughout the chocolate mass. Reserve a chunk of chocolate when melting the larger amount and set it aside.

3. Melt the chocolate until it registers 110–120°F.

Cooling Procedure

1. Once the proper melting temperature of the chocolate is achieved, replace the 120-degree water in the bottom of the double boiler with 95-degree water. Position the top vessel filled with melted chocolate over this water and cool, stirring occasionally, until it reaches 90–95°F. Remove the top vessel.

2. Add the reserved chunk of chocolate to the melted mass and continue to stir until its temperature reaches the following ranges:

    86–90°F. for bittersweet and semisweet chocolate
    83–88°F. for milk and white chocolate

3. Remove what is left of the chunk of chocolate and reserve it for subsequent cooling procedures. The chocolate is now in temper and ready to be used.

Maintaining the Temper

The bowl of tempered chocolate may be kept in temper for short periods of time only, by submerging it in another warm water bath. The temperature of the water this time must never be more than two degrees higher than the maximum temperature range allowed for tempered chocolate (see above).

How to Store Chocolate

Chocolate has a shelf life of at least one year under the proper storage conditions:

- Store in a tempered state.
- Store in a cool, dark, dry place (65–70°F., relative humidity of 50 percent or lower).
- Store chocolate well wrapped in plastic wrap or aluminum foil.
- *Do not* store near foreign flavors or odors.
- *Do not* store directly on floors or against walls to allow for breathing space.
- *Do not* store in the refrigerator.
- *Do not* store in the freezer.

5

Tips for Baking

- Baked goods are only as good as the ingredients that go into the products. Do not compromise with the quality of your ingredients and expect baked goods to turn out delicious.
- Read each recipe through twice before beginning to bake!
- Bring all ingredients to room temperature before beginning to bake.
- The flour used in the recipes in this book is all-purpose flour unless specified otherwise. Measure flour after sifting. Sifting lightens flour. To measure, scoop lightly into a dry measuring cup and level with a knife.
- Eggs are Grade A Large eggs unless specified otherwise.
  Eggs separate better when cold, but egg whites beat to greater volume when at room temperature. For even greater volume, clean out the egg white that sticks to the egg shell. When incorporating beaten egg whites into a batter, beat only until soft peaks form. When adding beaten egg whites to a mixture, stir in one-third to lighten it and then carefully fold in the rest.
- Unless a recipe indicates otherwise, *sugar* means granulated sugar. If granulated sugar is lumpy, sift it. Powdered sugar is the same as confectioner's sugar. If brown sugar has hardened, do not use it.
- Butter called for in recipes should be unsalted unless specified otherwise. Use butter at room temperature unless the recipe states otherwise. To soften butter quickly (even if frozen), put it through the grating or slicing disc of your food processor or use your microwave on the defrost setting. Use softened butter and a pastry brush to butter your baking pans and baking sheets. Generally, it is impossible to overcream butter and sugar; however, the rest of the ingredients should be added with a light hand.
- Cream referred to as *whipping cream* is also known as *heavy cream*. Chill cream well before attempting to whip it. When incorporating whipping cream into a batter, whip it only until soft mounds form. When adding whipped cream to a mixture, stir in a third of the whipped cream to lighten it and then carefully fold in the rest. To make firm whipping cream, for frosting or decorating a cake or pie, whip on the low speed of mixer for 5–10 minutes, increase speed, and whip until stiff.

- Use fresh baking powder, baking soda, and yeast. Check the expiration dates on the packages before using.
- Buy whole nuts. Roast them at 350°F. for 10–15 minutes, in a single layer, to bring out the flavor. If the nuts have skins, rub in a clean dish towel or shake in a sieve. Proceed to chop as directed in recipe. Freeze excess nuts until needed.
- Preheat oven for a full 15 minutes before baking. Be sure the oven is well regulated by using an oven thermometer. Begin to test recipes for doneness 5–10 minutes before suggested finishing times.
- Place pans in the center of the oven. If using several pans, stagger them. Do not bake in glass pans unless specified, because glass pans bake differently from metal ones. If using dark, well-seasoned pans, check baking times; recipes baked in dark pans will bake faster. If you don't have the size baking pans called for in a recipe, you may substitute other pans, as long as they hold the same volume. Should you wish to substitute a different-size pan even though you have the specified size, fill the substitute pan with water and then pour the water into the specified pan. If the substitute pan holds the same volume of water, you can use it. Baking times will change when pan size changes.
- Since recipes often call for lining pans with parchment paper, save time by precutting several rounds, squares, and rectangles in the sizes of your pans and keep them at hand.
- To fill baking pans evenly, use a scoop and add one scoop at a time to each pan until you've used up the mixture.

"THE DISCOVERY
of a new dish does more for
human happiness than the
discovery of a star."

Brillat-Savarin

6

The Choco-Chef's Kitchen

If you have the equipment listed below, you will be able to bake every recipe in this book. Much of it is necessary for the cook's kitchen, and some of it is special for the chocolate chef's kitchen. Top-quality equipment is an excellent investment as it will save the time and expense of frequent replacement. Brand-named products are suggested where they have superior attributes.

Small Tools

Dry and liquid measuring cups
Measuring spoons
Cake tester
Regular and offset long metal spatulas
Regular and offset short metal spatulas
Professional rubber spatulas, three
    lengths (Rubbermaid Professional)
Grater
Fine mesh strainer
Juicer
Zester
Wooden spoons
Professional whisks, several sizes
Ruler

Kitchen shears
Sifter
Chocolate dipping set (Wilton)
Rolling pin
Timer (West Bend)
Oven thermometer (Taylor)
Instant thermometer (Taylor)
Chocolate thermometer (Rose
    Beranbaum)
Candy thermometer (Rose
    Beranbaum)
Cookie cutter set, round
Pastry bag and tips (Wilton)
Chocolate chipper (Madame Chocolate)

All-Around Preparation

Scale (Terraillon)
Stainless steel mixing bowls
8-inch chef's knife (Henckels)
Long, thin serrated knife (Henckels)
Cutting board, polyethylene (Joyce
    Chen)
Small, heavy saucepan (Calphalon by
    Commercial Aluminum)

Medium, heavy saucepan (Calphalon
    by Commercial Aluminum)
Double boiler (Leyse Div., General
    Housewares Corp.)
Teapot
Cooling rack, large

Baking Pans

9-inch springform
10-inch springform
12-inch springform
8-inch-by-3-inch round cheesecake pan
3   8-inch-by-2-inch round cake pans
3   9-inch-by-3-inch round cake pans
8-inch-by-4-inch loaf pan
9-inch-by-13-inch baking pan
8-inch square cake pan

9-inch square cake pan
10-inch-by-15-inch jelly roll pan
Several 11-inch-by-14-inch baking
   sheets
9-inch tube pan
10-inch tube pan
1½-quart soufflé dish
Custard cups
Terrine (Le Crueset)

Electrics

Electric mixer with three bowls, two
   beaters, and two whips
   (Kitchenaid)

Food processor with two bowls, two
   steel knives (Cuisinart)
Microwave (Toshiba)

Paper Goods

Parchment paper
Waxed paper

Aluminum foil, professional-size roll
Plastic wrap, professional-size roll

"**I**N EATING
we experience a certain special
and indefinable well-being."
Brillat-Savarin

7

The Choco-Chef's Pantry

If you have the foods listed below in your pantry, you will be able to bake every recipe in this book. Brand names are listed where they have superior attributes.

Baking powder
Baking soda
Breadcrumbs
Butter, unsalted
Caramel (Nestlés, Madame Chocolate)
Chocolate (Madame Chocolate)
  Unsweetened
  Bittersweet
  Semisweet
  White
  Gianduja
  Orange Lait
  Bittersweet chocolate chunks
  Semisweet chocolate chunks
  Bittersweet chocolate chips
  Semisweet chocolate chips
  Milk chocolate chips
  Mint chocolate chips
  Mini semisweet chocolate chips
  Extra-large semisweet chocolate chips
  Extra-large milk chocolate chips
  Mint chocolate wafers
  Vermicelli
  Decor chips
Cinnamon

Cocoa, unsweetened
  Dutch Process
  (Madame Chocolate)
Coconut
Coffee
  Instant coffee powder
  Instant espresso
Cornstarch
Cream products
  Cream cheese
  Whipping cream
  Sour cream
  Crème Fraîche
Cream of tartar
Eggs, Grade A large
Extracts
  Pure almond
  Pure Vanilla (Neilsen-Massey)
  Pure chocolate
Flours
  All-purpose
  Cake
  Instant blending
  Bread
Food color

Fruit
  Cherries
  Strawberries
  Raspberries
  Lemons
  Oranges
  Pears
  Assorted glacéed
  Assorted dried
Gelatin, unflavored
Graham cracker crumbs
Liquors
  Amaretto
  Cognac
  Cointreau
  Crème de Cacao
  Frangelico
  Grand Marnier
  Kahlua
  Kirsch
  Rum
  Tia Maria
  Whiskey
  Poire
Marshmallows
  Mini
  Marshmallow cream
Milk and milk products
  Homogenized
  Buttermilk
  Sweet condensed
  Evaporated
  Yogurt
  Ricotta cheese

Nuts
  Almonds, whole
  Hazelnuts, whole (filberts)
  Pecans, whole
  Peanuts
  Walnuts, halves
Oils
  Almond (Kosto)
  Vegetable
Potato starch
Preserves, jellies, marmalades
  Red currant
  Raspberry
  Bitter orange
  Apricot
Raisins
Salt
Sugar
  Granulated
  Light brown
  Dark brown
  Powdered
  Superfine
Syrup
  Light corn
  Dark corn
Vanilla beans, whole (Neilsen-Massey)
Vinegar
Violets, candied
Wafers, chocolate
Wine
  Madeira
Yeast

"GOOD, WELL-MADE
chocolate can be assimilated
by any stomach which can
still digest even feebly."

Brillat-Savarin

8

Mousses, Puddings, and Fools

Mousses are a delight to behold, a joy to taste, and a treat to share with your dear ones. They will be deep in chocolate flavor if bittersweet chocolate is used and a little sweeter if semisweet chocolate is used. If you want an unusual mousse, substitute milk chocolate for the dark chocolate and your dessert will taste like a milk shake. The white chocolate mousses are delicious, too. There are times when I want people to experience the nuances of the different brands of chocolate (it's a very educating experience). Then I use the same recipe over and over, and all I do is change the brand of chocolate I use. A wine-tasting party, only with chocolate!

Tips for Making Mousse

- The most important tip I can give you for making mousses is not to overwhip your egg whites and whipping cream. They will fold in much easier if you take care to whip just until soft mounds form.
- Make sure all your ingredients are the same temperature (except for the whipping cream, which should be chilled). Warm chocolate will not combine with cold eggs. It will stiffen and be extremely hard to handle.
- Make your mousses early on the day you are going to use them; the taste will be much fresher. A mousse will pick up any strong odor present in your refrigerator.

Barbara Kafka's Chocolate Pôt de Crème

Barbara Kafka is an author, food and restaurant consultant, and cooking teacher. Some of my fondest memories are of the many times I spent in San Francisco with Barbara and James Beard—tasting. The experiences enable me to be discerning in the chocolate I choose. This is a light, but rich, end to a meal.

1⅓ cups semisweet
chocolate
6 Grade A large egg yolks
2 cups whipping cream
¼ cup sugar
1 teaspoon pure vanilla

Serves 8.

Beside all the obvious vessels (bowls, cups, glasses) one can use to serve mousse, you can also create your own vessel by molding it with tempered chocolate (see tempering in Index). You can mold in anything that is metal, stainless steel, or plastic. Glass cannot be used because it will not release the chocolate. Please make sure the object is food-safe.

1. Set aside 8 (½ cup) pôt de crème cups.

2. Prep work: Chop the chocolate fine and set aside. Lightly beat the yolks and set aside.

3. In a heavy saucepan, mix the cream and sugar together and scald by bringing it just to the boil. Remove from the heat; add the chocolate and stir until completely melted. Stir a small amount of the chocolate into the yolks to warm them slightly, and then pour the yolk mixture into the saucepan. Stir constantly, over medium heat, until thickened (about 3–5 minutes). Do not boil. Remove from heat and stir in vanilla. Pour into pôt de crème cups.

4. Chill cups in refrigerator before serving.

Pictured on color plate 2.

Dark Chocolate Mousse

THIS IS A VERY DENSE, satisfying mousse. It is made in the traditional style. It is the best way to satisfy my mother!

꿏

1. You will need a bowl or bowls for the finished mousse.

2. Prep work: Chop the chocolate into small pieces. Place the chocolate, sugar, and water in a heavy saucepan over low heat. Stir until mixture is melted and smooth. Remove from heat and set aside to cool. Separate the eggs and set the bowls aside.

3. In a mixer bowl, beat the yolks on high speed to the ribbon stage (about 3–5 minutes). Stir in the vanilla and then the chocolate mixture. Mix well. Beat whites until foamy; add the salt and beat to soft peaks. Fold a third of the whites into the chocolate mixture to lighten it, then fold in the remaining whites. Pour into serving dish.

4. Allow to chill overnight.

12 ounces bittersweet chocolate
½ cup sugar
⅓ cup water
5 Grade A large eggs
1 teaspoon pure vanilla
Pinch of salt

Serves 6.

Mousses can be scooped and served, much like ice cream, on a plate with a favorite piece of cake. They can be used as a filling between your favorite cake layers and can even be used to frost the cake.

Gabino Sotelino's White Chocolate Mousse

AMBRIA RESTAURANT, with Gabino Sotelino as its chef, is one of Chicago's finest. Dinner is always a treat when you can have Gabe's White Chocolate Mousse for dessert. Sometimes he serves it with a fresh raspberry sauce and other times with a chocolate sauce. The fresh lemon juice in this recipe heightens the taste of the white chocolate.

12 ounces white chocolate (do not use compound coating)
2 cups whipping cream
1 cup warm milk, divided
1 package unflavored gelatin
2 teaspoons pure vanilla
4 egg whites
Pinch of salt
Dash of lemon juice

Serves 12.

Gabino's recipe is served two ways at his restaurant, Ambria. One way is in a pool of fudge sauce and any of the recipes in my sauce chapter will work well. The other is in a pool of raspberry sauce (see Index). Apricot sauce can be made by thinning strained preserves with water, vanilla, or liqueur.

1. You must think about how you are going to serve the finished mousse. If you are using it on a buffet dessert table, then use a pretty glass bowl. It can also be divided into individual dessert bowls. Gabe, however, chills the mousse until it is firm in a stainless steel bowl. Then, using an oval scoop, he places three mounds of mousse in a pool of sauce on a dessert plate.

2. Prep work: Chop the white chocolate into small pieces and set aside. Chill the cream.

3. Melt the white chocolate in ¾ cup milk in the top of a double boiler over hot, not boiling, water. Stir until smooth; remove from heat and set aside. Soften gelatin in the remaining ¼ cup milk. Stir until it is smooth, placing the cup in hot water, if necessary. Add the softened gelatin to the melted chocolate and stir until it is very, very smooth. Remove from heat and stir in the vanilla. Allow it to cool to room temperature. Beat whites until foamy, add the salt, and beat to almost stiff peaks. Mix a third of the whites into the chocolate mixture. Gently fold in the rest in two batches. Whip the cream to soft mounds. Fold in the cream in three batches. Add the lemon juice and fold in. Pour into a serving bowl.

4. Allow to chill several hours before serving.

Pictured on color plate 2.

Leslee Reis's Mocha Mousse

LESLEE REIS IS THE CHEF/OWNER of two outstanding Evanston, Illinois, restaurants, Café Provençal and Leslee's. She is a wonderful chef and a great cooking teacher. Leslee created this mousse for one of Café Provençal's Signature Dinners on the regions of France. It combines two flavors: white chocolate and coffee.

1. You will need a serving bowl or small bowls for the finished mousse.

2. Prep work: Grate the white chocolate and set aside. Combine the espresso and hot water, stir, and set aside.

3. In the top of a double boiler, off the heat, beat the yolks, sugar, and salt until pale yellow and creamy. Place top of double boiler into bottom and bring to a gentle simmer. Gradually add madeira, beating constantly with a whisk, until mixture swells into a light, soft mass. Continue whisking until custard (Sabayon) forms soft mounds like thick pudding. Remove from heat. Stir in white chocolate until smooth. Stir in 1 tablespoon espresso, or more to taste. Allow mixture to cool. Whip the cream to soft mounds. Mix a third into the mousse to lighten it and carefully fold in the rest. Pour into bowls.

4. Allow to chill for several hours. (This mousse can also be used as the filling for a cake, if desired).

10 ounces white chocolate (do not use compound coating)
1 tablespoon powdered espresso coffee (or more to taste)
1 tablespoon hot water (or more)
5 grade A large egg yolks
½ cup sugar
Pinch of salt
6 tablespoons dry madeira
2 cups whipping cream

Serves 8.

The flavors of both chocolate and coffee come from the roasting of seeds of tropical plants. This creates a natural bridge whereby the flavor of one complements the flavor of the other.

Amaretto Chocolate Mousse

38

ALMOND IS ANOTHER FLAVOR that goes well with chocolate, and this mousse is especially smooth and tasty.

❧

*6 ounces semisweet
    chocolate*
*1 ounce unsweetened
    chocolate*
8 Grade A large eggs
*2 tablespoons amaretto
    liqueur*
¼ teaspoon salt
*Grated semisweet
    chocolate for garnish*

Serves 6.

1. You will need a serving bowl or small bowls for the finished mousse.

2. Prep work: Chop the chocolates into small pieces and melt in the top of a double boiler over hot, not boiling, water. Stir until smooth and remove from the heat. Set aside. Separate the eggs and set the bowls aside.

3. In a mixer bowl, beat the yolks until thick and light. Stir in the chocolates and the amaretto. (If you desire, you can use the liqueur of your choice instead of amaretto.) Blend well. Beat the whites until foamy; add the salt; beat to soft peaks. Mix a third of whites into chocolate mixture to lighten it, then carefully fold in the rest. Pour into the serving bowl.

4. Allow to chill for several hours. Garnish with the grated chocolate.

You can mold your own vessel for the mousse from melted, tempered chocolate, if you like. That way you can have your mousse and eat its plate, too!

White Chocolate Strawberry Mousse

THIS COMBINATION of white chocolate and strawberry is wonderful when fresh berries are available. It is a delicious treat made with frozen strawberries.

1. You will need a serving bowl or small bowls for the finished mousse.

2. Prep work: Chop the white chocolate into small pieces. Place in the top of a double boiler over hot, not boiling, water. Stir until smooth and set aside. Stir the lemon juice into the strawberry puree and set aside. Stir the gelatin into the boiling water. Stir to dissolve and set aside to cool. Chill the cream.

3. In a large bowl, stir the gelatin into the strawberry mixture. Add the sweetened condensed milk and the melted white chocolate. Stir to blend well. Whip the cream to soft mounds. Mix a third of the cream into the white chocolate mixture to lighten it, then carefully fold in the rest. Pour into serving bowls.

4. Allow to chill several hours.

8 ounces white chocolate (do not use compound coating)

2 tablespoons fresh lemon juice

2 cups strawberry puree

2 envelopes unflavored gelatin

1/4 cup boiling water

1/2 cup sweetened condensed milk

1 cup whipping cream

Serves 8–10.

Serve this in a cup made out of melted, tempered chocolate. It will be eye-appealing as well as delicious.

Chocolate Mousse

A SIMPLE NAME for a simple but sensuous recipe. This is my favorite chocolate mousse recipe because it does not contain any sugar or vanilla. All you taste is the deep, dark taste of fine chocolate.

16 ounces bittersweet, semisweet, or milk chocolate
8 Grade A large eggs
⅛ teaspoon salt
2⅔ cups whipping cream

Serves 12.

Have a chocolate mousse tasting party. To taste the differences in the many available brands of chocolate, prepare this recipe four times using a different chocolate each time. The nuances that appear from brand to brand really come through.

1. You will need a serving bowl or small bowls for the finished mousse.

2. Prep work: Chop the chocolate into small pieces and set aside. Place chocolate in the top of a double boiler over hot, not boiling, water. Stir until smooth; remove from the heat and set aside to cool. Separate 5 of the eggs. Add the remaining 3 whole eggs to the bowl of yolks. Set the bowls aside. Chill the cream.

3. Make sure the eggs and yolks are at room temperature. Whisk the eggs until blended. Slowly add the chocolate. If the eggs are too cold or the chocolate too hot, the mixture will be impossible to stir. If this happens, set the bowl over hot water to warm the mixture for a few minutes. Beat the whites until foamy; add the salt and continue beating until soft peaks form. Mix a third of the whites into the chocolate mixture. Fold in the remaining whites in 2 batches. Whip the cream to soft mounds. Fold into the chocolate mixture in 3 batches. Pour into serving bowl.

4. Allow to chill at least 2 hours or until firm.

Pictured on color plate 2.

Baked Chocolate Rice Pudding

MARION CUNNINGHAM is known as "Fannie Farmer." She is the author of the recent revision of the *Fannie Farmer Baking Book*. You'll love this easy rice pudding she was gracious enough to share.

1. Preheat oven to 300°F. Butter an 8-inch square baking pan and set aside.

2. Prep work: Chop the chocolate into small pieces and place in the top of a double boiler over hot, not boiling, water. Stir until smooth and remove from the heat.

3. Put all the ingredients in the prepared pan and stir well to blend.

4. Bake 3½ hours, stirring 3 times during the first hour of baking so the rice doesn't settle. Serve warm or cold with whipping cream, if desired.

2 ounces unsweetened chocolate
4 cups milk
½ teaspoon salt
⅔ cup sugar
3 tablespoons long grain rice
Whipping cream (optional)

Serves 6–8.

Chocolate Strawberry Fool

A FOOL IS A FRUIT DISH that originated in England and has been adopted by Americans. In this very simple and great-tasting dessert, dark chocolate and strawberries are combined. It is a perfect family treat and easy enough for children to prepare.

1. You will need 8 dessert bowls for the finished fool.

2. Prep work: Chill the cream. Grate the chocolate and set aside. Place the strawberries in a strainer and drain well. Set aside.

3. In a mixer bowl, beat the cream and salt to soft peaks. Add the sugar and beat just until firm. (Keeping the cream on the soft side makes the texture of the fool better.) Gently fold in the grated chocolate and the strawberries. Spoon into the dessert bowls.

4. This dessert should be served immediately or may be chilled for up to 30 minutes.

2 cups whipping cream
4 ounces semisweet chocolate
2 10-ounce packages frozen strawberries
⅛ teaspoon salt
⅓ cup sugar

Serves 8.

9

Cakes

There is no better way to celebrate an event than with a chocolate cake! As we retested the recipes in this chapter, the cakes kept getting better and better. Start at the beginning and bake your way through the chapter. Have a wonderful chocolate cake party. There are easy-to-bake cakes and others that require time and patience. Whichever one you choose, you will not be disappointed. Each and every cake is rich and extremely delicious. In any of the recipes calling for bittersweet or semisweet chocolate the other may be substituted. Bittersweet chocolate will give you a more intense chocolate taste.

- Measure ingredients carefully for best results.
- Use a quality oven thermometer to determine how well the oven is regulated.
- Do not substitute pan sizes and expect the baking time to remain the same.
- Bake cake layers in the center of the oven, being sure that pans are not touching each other or the oven walls. This allows for proper heat circulation.
- A cake is done when you press the top gently and it springs back without any imprint left, when a cake tester inserted in the center (or wherever the recipe directs) has a dry crumb, and when the cake pulls away from the side of the pan.
- If a chocolate cake requires refrigeration, allow at least 30 minutes to return to room temperature before serving. The chocolate flavor will be more intense.

If Something Goes Wrong with Your Cake

Collapsed Center	*Overflowing Pan*
Too much sugar	Pan too small
Too little baking powder	Batter unevenly divided
Underbaking	Oven racks not level

Lopsided Cake

Oven shelves not level
Pans touching one another
 or oven walls

Heavy Cake

Too much sugar
Too little baking powder
Excessive beating
Removed from oven before
 completely baked

Cracked Top

Too much flour
Oven temperature too high

Sticky Top

Too much sugar

Too Coarse

Too much shortening
Too much baking powder
Underbaking
Oven temperature too low

Uneven Texture

Undermixing

Dry Cake

Too much flour
Too little shortening
Overbaking

Uneven Browning

Oven not preheated
Oven temperature too high
Pans crowded

Simple Flourless Chocolate Cake

THIS IS A RECIPE that will be an oft-baked favorite. It has a great taste and is quick to prepare. It is easy enough to make for tonight's dinner.

✲

1. Preheat oven to 250°F. Butter and flour a 9-inch springform pan and set aside.

2. Prep work: Carefully separate eggs and set bowls aside. Chop the chocolate into small pieces and melt with the butter in the top of a double boiler over hot, not boiling, water. When the chocolate is melted, remove the pot from the heat and cool to room temperature. (Be sure the mixture is smooth by stirring frequently.)

3. Beat the whites until foamy. Slowly add the sugar and beat until stiff. Mix yolks with a whisk and then stir into the chocolate mixture. Add the whites to the chocolate mixture and fold in carefully. Pour the batter into the prepared pan and smooth the top.

4. Bake for 1 hour and 15 minutes.

5. Cool cake in the pan. Remove the sides. Just before serving, sprinkle top with powdered sugar. (This cake can be frozen if wrapped well, first in plastic wrap and then in aluminum foil.)

7 Grade A large eggs
10 ounces semisweet chocolate
7 tablespoons unsalted butter at room temperature
⅓ cup sugar
Powdered sugar for garnish

Serves 8–10.

Having few ingredients other than chocolate, this cake is excellent for comparing brands of chocolate. Nestlé's Burgundy, Guittard French Vanilla, Ghirardelli Queen, Lindt Excellence, Carma Bourbon-Vanilla, and Callebaut Semisweet are high-quality brands.

Jean Banchet's Gâteau au Chocolat

L E FRANÇAIS IS ONE of America's top-rated restaurants. The imagination and talent of its chef/owner, Jean Banchet, know no bounds. This recipe, one of my favorites, is a very rich cake and will serve a lot of people. Jean has also included his recipe for Crème Anglaise, which should be placed in a pool around each slice of cake.

14 ounces bittersweet chocolate
10 Grade A large eggs
¾ cup plus 2 tablespoons unsalted butter, room temperature
1½ cups sugar, divided
1 tablespoon Grand Marnier
1 teaspoon pure vanilla
Powdered sugar to garnish (optional)
Crème Anglaise (optional) (recipe follows)

Serves 12–16.

Have an international cake party! Complement the cakes with interesting coffees. Bake Elaine González's Torta Mexicana, Doris Banchet's Italian Torte, and Jean Banchet's Gâteau au Chocolat.

1. Preheat oven to 250°F. Butter and flour a 12-inch springform pan and set aside.

2. Prep work: Chop the chocolate into small pieces so it will melt quickly. Set aside. Carefully separate the eggs and set bowls aside.

3. Melt the chocolate and butter in the top of a double boiler over hot, not boiling, water. Stir the mixture occasionally until it is smooth. Add 1¼ cups of the sugar and stir until it is almost dissolved. Beat the yolks in a separate bowl. Beat half of the hot mixture into the yolks, a little at a time. When egg yolk mixture is smooth, add it back into the remaining hot mixture. Cook, stirring constantly, until the mixture becomes slightly thickened. Stir in Grand Marnier and vanilla. Remove from the heat and cool slightly. In a separate bowl, beat the egg whites to soft peaks, gradually adding the remaining sugar; then beat to stiff peaks. Pour the chocolate mixture over the whites and fold together carefully. Pour the batter into the prepared pan and smooth with a small spatula.

4. Bake the cake for 3 hours.

5. Allow the cake to cool in the pan until it reaches room temperature. Cover with plastic wrap and chill. When ready to serve, remove the sides from the pan and place cake on a platter. Sift powdered sugar over the top if desired. For a very pretty effect, place a doily on the top of the cake and gently sift powdered sugar over it. Remove it carefully, and the design will remain on the cake. Serve with Crème Anglaise, if desired. (This cake can be frozen if wrapped well, first in plastic wrap and then in aluminum foil.)

Crème Anglaise

1. Use a heavy saucepan to make this sauce.

2. In a mixer bowl, beat the egg yolks lightly and set aside.

3. In the heavy saucepan, bring the milk to a boil and remove from the heat. Add the sugar to the egg yolks and beat until light. Whisk a small amount of the hot milk at a time into the yolks to warm them. When yolks are warm, return the egg mixture to the saucepan and add the vanilla beans. Place over moderate heat, stirring constantly, until the custard coats a spoon. Do not allow to boil. Strain the custard into a clean bowl. Set the bowl in a pan of ice water to cool. Refrigerate the leftovers.

8 egg yolks
1 quart milk
1¼ cups sugar
2 whole vanilla beans

Crème Anglaise is a thickened custard sauce which may also be served with fresh fruit, ice cream, and soufflés. A variety of tastes can be had by adding coffee, melted chocolate, or liqueur to the hot liquid while preparing the sauce.

The Cottage Chocolate Mousse Cake

THIS RECIPE COMES from the talented chef/ owner of "The Cottage" restaurant in Calumet City, Illinois. Carolyn Buster is a wonderful baker as well as a fabulous cook. Her restaurant is one of my favorites. This intricate recipe requires patience, but is worth the time involved. The cake in this recipe is delicious all by itself.

1½ cups Clarified Butter (recipe follows)
1 cup all-purpose flour
1 cup unsweetened cocoa
12 Grade A large eggs
2 cups sugar
2 teaspoons pure vanilla
Chocolate Mousse Filling (recipe follows)
Chocolate Glaze (recipe follows)
Whipped cream to garnish

Serves 12–14.

Although Carolyn's cake is delicious as it is, you may substitute any of the other mousses in this book for the chocolate one listed in this recipe. You will have created your own cake and it will be most delicious!

1. Preheat oven to 350°F. Butter a 14-inch-by-17-inch cake pan. Cut parchment paper to fit the bottom and butter the paper. Flour the lined pan and set aside. Lightly oil a 10-inch-by-3-inch springform pan and set aside.

2. Prep work: Clarify the butter (instructions follow) and set aside. Sift the flour and cocoa together and set aside. Separate the eggs and set the bowls aside.

3. In a mixer bowl, beat the egg yolks, gradually adding the sugar. Beat until thick and fluffy. Beat in the vanilla. Sift the flour/cocoa mixture into the egg mixture and fold in thoroughly, using a large rubber spatula. The batter will be very stiff. Beat the whites to stiff peaks. Mix a third of the whites into the batter to lighten it, then gently but thoroughly, fold in the rest. Place about 2 cups of the batter in a small bowl and thoroughly fold in all of the clarified butter. Return this mixture back into the rest of the batter and fold it all together. Pour batter into the prepared cake pan and smooth top.

4. Bake 20–25 minutes or until a toothpick inserted in the center comes out clean.

5. Cool cake in the pan. Invert onto a cake rack and slice horizontally into two layers. Using the layers, cut the cake to line the bottom and sides of the prepared springform pan. Fill with Chocolate Mousse Filling and cover with remaining cake slices. Cover and refrigerate at least 24 hours. Uncover and remove the sides of the pan. Place your serving plate over the cake; invert and remove the bottom of the pan. Place strips of waxed paper under the cake so the glaze will not mess your plate. Pour Chocolate Glaze over cake, using a small spatula to

smooth sides. Remove waxed paper. Slice and serve with a dollop of whipped cream. This cake is extremely rich and should be served in very small slices. It may serve more than the 14 suggested. (Either the plain cake or the finished cake can be frozen, provided you wrap it well, first with plastic wrap and then with aluminum foil.)

Chocolate Mousse Filling

1. Prep work: Separate eggs and set the bowls aside. Chop the chocolate into small pieces and melt in the coffee in the top of a double boiler over hot, not boiling, water. Remove from the heat, place in a medium bowl and set aside.

2. In the bowl of your mixer, beat the yolks until pale yellow and thick. Blend yolks into the chocolate mixture; gradually add the liqueur and allow mixture to cool. In separate bowls beat the whites to stiff peaks; whip the cream to soft peaks. Mix a third of the egg whites into the chocolate mixture to lighten it and then gently fold in the remaining whites and the whipped cream.

4 Grade A large eggs
2 pounds bittersweet chocolate
½ cup prepared strong coffee
½ cup Tia Maria liqueur
½ cup whipping cream

Chocolate Glaze

1. Prep work: Cut the butter into pieces and set aside.
2. In a saucepan, mix the sugar, cocoa, and water; bring to a boil. Cook, stirring constantly, until slightly thickened and the mixture coats the back of a spoon (about 3–5 minutes). Remove from heat and gradually whisk in the butter pieces. Whisk until smooth.

½ cup plus 5 tablespoons unsalted butter at room temperature
¾ cups sugar
4 tablespoons unsweetened cocoa
½ cup water

Clarified Butter

Place the butter in the top of a double boiler over low heat for 45 minutes. At the end of that time the butter will have separated into three distinct layers. The top layer should be skimmed off with a spoon and discarded. The middle layer is the pure butterfat. This should be ladled into the necessary vessel, being careful that the milk solids of the bottom layer do not get into the ladle. Butter can be clarified in quantity and stored in a mason jar. It will keep indefinitely in your refrigerator.

2 cups unsalted butter

Alice Medrich's Chocolate Hazelnut Torte

ALICE MEDRICH is the owner of my favorite French pastry and chocolate specialty shop. Unfortunately for me, Cocolat is located in Berkeley, California, and I can't get there as often as I would like. However, I never come home without a shopping bag full of goodies. This Cocolat specialty is one of my favorites.

6 ounces bittersweet
  chocolate
¾ cup unsalted butter at
  room temperature
4 Grade A large eggs
½ cup hazelnuts
¼ cup all-purpose flour
¾ cup sugar, divided
⅛ teaspoon almond
  extract
Pinch of salt
⅛ teaspoon cream of
  tartar
Chocolate Glaze (recipe
  follows)

Serves 8–10.

1. Preheat the oven to 350°F. Butter an 8-inch round cake pan. Cut parchment paper to fit the bottom and butter the paper. Flour the lined pan and set aside.

2. Prep work: Chop the chocolate into small pieces and place in the top of a double boiler with the butter. Place over hot, not boiling, water and stir until smooth. Remove from the heat and set aside. Separate the eggs and set the bowls aside. Toast the hazelnuts in a 350°F. oven for approximately 15 minutes. Cool and chop fine in a food processor. Set aside. Sift the flour and set aside.

3. In a large bowl, whisk the egg yolks with ½ cup of the sugar until the mixture is pale and forms a ribbon. Stir in the almond extract, the melted chocolate, the nuts, and the flour, until smooth. Beat the egg whites until foamy, adding the salt and cream of tartar. When soft peaks form, add the remaining ¼ cup sugar and beat to firm, not stiff peaks. Mix about a third of the egg whites into the chocolate mixture to lighten it and then quickly fold in the remaining whites. Pour the batter into the prepared pan and smooth the top.

4. Bake 40–45 minutes or until a toothpick inserted 1 inch from the edge of the pan reveals a dry crumb. The center should be wet but not runny.

5. Cool the cake in the pan. Press top of cake down to make it level and turn out onto a serving plate. Remove the parchment paper. Place strips of wax paper around the cake and pour the chocolate glaze over the cake. Smooth the sides with a small spatula. (This cake freezes beautifully, preferably without the glaze. To freeze, be sure the cake is well wrapped, first with plastic wrap and then with aluminum foil.)

Chocolate Glaze

Chop the chocolate into small pieces and melt with the butter in the top of a double boiler over hot, not boiling, water. Remove from heat and stir in the cognac.

6 ounces bittersweet chocolate
½ cup unsalted butter at room temperature
1 tablespoon cognac

Do not be afraid to substitute frostings or glaze to suit your taste.

Susie Skoog's Chocolate Cherry Cake

CHOCOLATE AND CHERRIES are a delicious combination, and this cake shows this off! Susie is an expert baker and an expert at combining flavors.

⁂

8 ounces semisweet chocolate
1 cup (1 pound) pitted tart cherries
4 Grade A large eggs
¼ cup Kirsch (cherry brandy)
¾ pound unsalted butter, very soft
⅓ cup all-purpose flour
⅓ cup sugar
Chocolate Ganache (see index)

Serves 8–10.

1. Preheat oven to 375°F. Cut parchment paper to fit the bottom of a 9-inch round cake pan and set aside.

2. Prep work: Chop the chocolate fine and set aside. Separate the eggs and set the bowls aside. Drain the cherries well, chop them, and set aside.

3. Place the chocolate and kirsch in the top of a double boiler over hot, not boiling, water. Stir until smooth and remove the top part from the heat. Stir in the yolks, one at a time. Return the pan to the heat and whisk for a minute or two until the yolks are warmed. Remove from the heat and whisk in the very soft butter. Then whisk in the flour and cherries. Beat the egg whites to soft peaks. Gradually add the sugar while beating to soft meringue peaks. (Do not overbeat!) Mix a third of the egg whites into the chocolate mixture to lighten it. Fold in the remaining whites. Pour batter into the prepared pan and smooth the top.

4. Bake 25–30 minutes or until a toothpick inserted 1 inch from the edge of the pan reveals a moist crumb. The center of the cake will be creamy.

5. Cool the cake in the pan on a rack. Run a knife around the edge of the pan and invert the cake onto a serving plate. Remove the parchment paper. Frost with Chocolate Ganache. (Cake freezes beautifully provided it is properly wrapped, first with plastic wrap and then with aluminum foil.)

Chocolate Chip Kahlua Torte

AN EASY-TO-MAKE TORTE that is quite different and very, very good. The chocolate chips spread the chocolate taste throughout the torte without oversweetening the dessert.

❉

1. Preheat oven to 350°F. Butter a 9-inch springform pan and set aside.

2. Prep work: Chop the walnuts and set aside.

3. In a mixer bowl, beat the eggs on medium speed and slowly add the sugar. Beat until light and fluffy. Add the graham cracker crumbs, the baking powder, and the Kahlua. Mix very well. Add chocolate chips and walnuts and blend thoroughly. Spread into the prepared pan.

4. Bake exactly 30 minutes.

5. Cool on a cake rack. Remove sides of springform pan and frost top with Kahlua Frosting. (Cake can be frozen without the frosting, provided it is wrapped well, first in plastic wrap and then in aluminum foil.)

Kahlua Frosting

Beat all ingredients together until soft peaks form.

1 cup walnuts
3 Grade A large eggs
1 cup sugar
2 cups graham cracker crumbs
1 teaspoon baking powder
2 tablespoons Kahlua
1 cup semisweet chocolate chips
Kahlua Frosting (recipe follows)

Serves 8.

1 cup heavy cream
1 tablespoon sugar
¼ cup Kahlua

Vary either the sweetness or size of the chocolate chips used in the Kahlua Torte and the cake will taste different each time.

Chocolate Marquise with Espresso Sauce

THIS RECIPE CAME from the *Chicago Tribune* Test Kitchen. It is the creation of the test kitchen director, Jean Marie Brownson. The use of both chocolate and cocoa makes it extra chocolaty. You may eat a good deal of the filling before you even put it into the ladyfingers—it's delicious!

5 ounces semisweet chocolate
2 cups whipping cream
1 3-ounce package ladyfingers (it will be better if you bake your own)
Brandy or dark rum
7 Grade A large egg yolks
1 cup sugar
1 cup plus 5 tablespoons unsalted butter at room temperature
1⅓ cups unsweetened Dutch process cocoa
Sweetened whipped cream for garnish
Espresso Sauce (recipe follows)

Serves 8.

1. Line the bottom and sides of a 1½-quart soufflé dish with waxed paper.

2. Prep work: Chop the chocolate into small pieces and melt in the top of a double boiler over hot, not boiling, water. Stir until smooth and set aside. Line the bottom of the soufflé dish with ladyfingers to resemble a flower. Line the sides of the dish with ladyfingers, cutting them, if necessary, to make them fit. Sprinkle them with brandy or rum and set aside.

3. In a mixer bowl, beat the yolks, gradually adding the sugar until they are light and fluffy (about 2 minutes). Stir the warm, melted chocolate into the yolk mixture. In another bowl, cream the butter until light and fluffy. Gradually beat in the cocoa, stopping the mixer to scrape down the bowl after each addition. Mix the butter mixture into the yolk mixture until it is very smooth. In a separate bowl, whip the cream to soft peaks. Stir in a third of the whipped cream. Fold in the remaining cream until all the ingredients are mixed. Spoon into the soufflé dish (or into your mouth). Trim any ladyfingers that extend above the mold.

4. Refrigerate, covered, at least 4 hours.

5. Place a serving dish over the Marquise and invert. Remove waxed paper. Garnish with sweetened whipped cream. To serve, spoon some of the Espresso Sauce around the Marquise and serve the rest in a separate sauceboat.

Espresso Sauce

Mix milk and sugar in a heavy saucepan and heat to the boil. Stir until the sugar dissolves. Stir in the coffee powder. In a separate bowl, whisk the egg yolks until they are light and lemon-colored. Pour some of the hot milk mixture into the yolks to warm them. Return the mixture to the saucepan. Cook over medium heat, stirring constantly, until the mixture coats a spoon and registers 180°F. on an instant-reading thermometer. Do not boil. Remove from the heat and allow to cool, stirring frequently. Cover and refrigerate for up to 3 days.

1 cup milk
5 tablespoons sugar
1 tablespoon instant
  espresso coffee
3 Grade A large egg yolks

Serves 8–10.

Experiment with espresso, various strengths of brewed coffee, coffee syrup, or Kahlua to vary the flavor of recipes containing coffee.

Susie Skoog's Chocolate Whiskey Cake

Susie Skoog IS A VERY special friend. She's a professional baker and is a dessert consultant for many of Chicago's fine restaurants. She trained at Berkeley's renowned Cocolat Bakery. Many of her delicious recipes are in this book because of her willingness to share her creations.

½ *cup seedless raisins*
¼ *cup whiskey*
6 *ounces semisweet*
  chocolate
½ *cup unsalted butter at*
  room temperature
⅔ *cup sugar*
3 *Grade A large eggs*
¼ *cup breadcrumbs*
5 *ounces ground almonds*
Chocolate Ganache
  (recipe follows)

Serves 8–10.

1. Preheat oven to 375°F. Butter an 8-inch round cake pan. Cut parchment paper to fit the bottom and butter the paper. Flour the lined pan and set aside.

2. Prep work: Combine the raisins and whiskey and marinate at least 1 hour or overnight. Chop the chocolate into small pieces and melt in a double boiler over hot, not boiling, water. Stir until smooth and set aside.

3. In a mixer bowl, cream the butter until fluffy. Gradually add the sugar, beating at moderate speed. Add the eggs, one at a time, beating well. Stop the mixer after beating in each egg and, with a rubber spatula, scrape down the sides of the bowl. With the mixer on low speed, add the chocolate, breadcrumbs, almonds, raisins, and whiskey. Beat only until combined. Pour the batter into the prepared cake pan and smooth the top.

4. Bake 25 minutes or until a toothpick inserted 1 inch from the edge of the pan has a dry crumb. The center of the cake will still be wet.

5. Cool the cake in the pan on a rack. Invert cake onto rack and set over a baking sheet. Pour Chocolate Ganache over the top of cake. Use a small spatula to push ganache over the sides of the cake. Smooth the top and sides with the spatula. Eat the extra ganache right off the spatula. (Cake freezes beautifully, provided it is properly wrapped, first with plastic wrap and then with aluminum foil.)

Chocolate Ganache

1. Prep work: Chop the chocolate into small pieces and set aside.

2. In a heavy saucepan, scald the cream (bring it just to the boiling point). Remove from heat; add the chocolate and whisk until smooth. Cool until thickened but still pourable. Any remaining ganache can be frozen.

8 ounces semisweet chocolate
1 cup whipping cream

This cake can be varied to suit the taste buds. Bourbon, scotch, or any blended whiskey may be used to produce this cake's unique flavor. Any dried or glacéed fruit can be substituted for the raisins.

White Chocolate Cake

THIS IS AN OLD-FASHIONED cake, a recipe that I've had for many years. Today there is a broad choice in the brands of white chocolate. The cake will have a subtle flavor unlike that of a dark chocolate cake. The frosting was created by Rose Levy Beranbaum who runs the Cordon Rose Cooking School in New York City.

2½ *cups cake flour*
1 *teaspoon baking soda*
⅓ *cup white chocolate (do not use compound coating)*
½ *cup hot water*
4 *Grade A large eggs*
1 *cup unsalted butter at room temperature*
1½ *cups sugar*
1 *teaspoon pure vanilla*
1 *cup buttermilk*
Pinch of salt
Rose Levy Beranbaum's White Chocolate Frosting (recipe follows)

Serves 10–12.

1. Preheat the oven to 350°F. Grease and flour three 9-inch cake pans and set aside.

2. Prep work: Sift the cake flour and baking soda together and set aside. Chop the white chocolate into small pieces and melt in ½ cup hot water in the top of a double boiler over hot, not boiling, water. Stir until smooth, remove from heat, and cool. Separate the eggs and set the bowls aside.

3. In a mixer bowl, cream the butter and sugar until light and fluffy. Add the yolks, one at a time, beating well after each addition. Blend in the white chocolate and the vanilla. Add the flour mixture and buttermilk, alternately, to the creamed mixture. Beat whites until foamy. Add a pinch of salt and beat the whites on high speed until stiff peaks form. Mix a quarter of the whites into the creamed mixture to lighten it, then carefully fold in the remainder. Divide the batter evenly among the 3 prepared pans. Smooth tops.

4. Bake 25–30 minutes.

5. Cool cake layers on a rack. Frost with White Chocolate Frosting. (While the cake layers can be frozen, best results will be obtained by frosting the cake on the day it is served. Be sure the layers are well wrapped, first with plastic wrap and then aluminum foil.)

Rose Levy Beranbaum's White Chocolate Frosting

1. Prep work: Chop the white chocolate into small pieces and set aside.

2. Melt the white chocolate in the remaining ingredients in the top of a double boiler over hot, not boiling, water. Remove from the heat and stir until smooth. Pour the mixture into a mixing bowl and place over a bowl of water and ice cubes sprinkled with 2 tablespoons salt. Whisk only until whisk marks appear in the mixture. Remove from the cold water. Frosting should be soft when used to frost the cake. (Frosting can be frozen indefinitely. If it hardens, soften it over hot water.)

1½ pounds white chocolate (do not use compound coating)
¼ cup cocoa butter
5 tablespoons unsalted Clarified Butter (see index)
¼ cup flavorless vegetable oil

Makes 2½ cups.

Use pure vanilla made from vanilla beans soaked in alcohol. The finest vanilla is made from the natural Madagascar bean the Neilsen-Massey Company manufactures. It is available in double strength from Madame Chocolate.

Elaine González's Torta Mexicana

ELAINE'S WONDERFUL BOOK, *Chocolate Artistry* (Contemporary Books, Inc.), is an ideal companion to this book. Using chocolate as an art form, these desserts can look spectacular. Her book will show you how to do it. She is a talented artist and an accomplished baker—as shown by this uniquely delicious cake. ⚜

2½ *cups cake flour*
¼ *teaspoon salt*
1 *teaspoon baking soda*
1 *teaspoon ground cinnamon*
½ *cup Dutch process cocoa*
5 *Grade A large eggs*
1 *cup unsalted butter at room temperature*
2 *cups sugar*
1 *cup sour cream*
¼ *cup Kahlua*
1 *teaspoon pure vanilla*
Kahlua Mousse Filling *(recipe follows)*
Kahlua Buttercream Icing *(recipe follows)*

Serves 12–16.

1. Preheat the oven to 350°F. Butter a 12-inch round, 2-inch-deep cake pan. Cut parchment paper to fit the bottom of the pan and grease the paper. Flour the lined pan and set aside.

2. Prep work: Sift the cake flour, salt, baking soda, cinnamon, and cocoa together at least three times to blend thoroughly. In a small bowl, blend the sour cream, Kahlua, and vanilla and set aside. Separate the eggs and set the bowls aside. Cut the butter into small pieces and set aside.

3. In a mixer bowl, at moderate speed, beat the yolks until thick and creamy. In a separate bowl, cream the butter, adding sugar gradually until well blended. Add creamed mixture to yolks; beat thoroughly. Reduce speed and alternately add the flour mixture and sour cream mixture. Beat only until blended after each addition. Beat whites to stiff, not dry, peaks. Fold whites into batter in three additions. Pour batter into pan and smooth top.

4. Bake 55 minutes.

5. Cool cake in pan for about 5 minutes before inverting onto a rack to cool completely. Slide a 12-inch cardboard round under the cake. Slice the cake horizontally to make 2 layers. Spread Kahlua Mousse Filling to within ¼ inch of edge of cake. Top with other layer, crumb side down. Smooth excess mousse from sides of cake using a spatula, if necessary. Chill cake for several hours. Ice cake with a thick coating of Kahlua Buttercream Icing to conceal dark surface of the cake. Decorate top as desired. (Cake layers freeze well, provided they are

well wrapped, first in plastic wrap and then in aluminum foil. Fill and frost the cake the day you wish to serve
it.)

Kahlua Mousse

Chop the chocolate into small pieces and place in the
top of a double boiler over hot, not boiling, water. Stir
until smooth, remove from heat, and allow to cool 10
minutes. Sprinkle cream of tartar over egg whites; beat to
stiff, not dry, peaks. Beat cream on low speed until it begins to thicken. Increase speed and beat until thick. Mix
in the Kahlua and vanilla. Whisk 1½ cups of whites into
remaining whites. Fold in whipped cream. Use to fill
cooled cake.

*8 ounces semisweet
  chocolate*
*⅛ teaspoon cream of
  tartar*
*4 Grade A large egg
  whites*
2 cups whipping cream
5 tablespoons Kahlua
2 tablespoons vanilla

Kahlua Buttercream

1. Cut the butter into pieces and set aside. Sift the
powdered sugar and set aside.

2. Cream the butter and shortening. Gradually add
powdered sugar, mixing well. In a saucepan over medium heat, stir the milk and cornstarch until thickened
like pudding. Pour in a mixer bowl; beat until cooled,
about 7 minutes. Add creamed butter to cooled mixture
by heaping spoonfuls, blending well after each addition.
Add flavorings; mix briefly. (Overbeating softens icing.)
Use to ice cake.

*1½ cups unsalted butter at
  room temperature*
2 cups powdered sugar
*½ cup white vegetable
  shortening*
2 cups milk
6 tablespoons cornstarch
2 teaspoons pure vanilla
2 teaspoons Kahlua

62

Chocolate Truffle Torte

ROSE LEVY BERANBAUM is a New York chocolate artist. Aside from wedding cakes, for which she is noted, she has also created this rich, smooth chocolate torte complemented with a raspberry sauce. This recipe was developed by Rose for the Poulain Chocolate Company for use with Poulain chocolate.

7 ounces Poulain bittersweet chocolate (20 logs)
½ cup unsalted butter at room temperature
3 Grade A large eggs
Whipped cream for garnish
Raspberry Sauce (recipe follows)

Serves 8–10.

1. Preheat the oven to 425°F. Cut parchment paper to fit the bottom of an 8-inch-by-4-inch loaf pan with a 4-cup capacity. Butter and flour the sides of the pan.

2. Prep work: Chop the chocolate into small pieces and melt with the butter in the top of a double boiler over hot, not boiling, water. Allow mixture to cool slightly.

3. In a large mixing bowl set over, not in, simmering water, stir the eggs until they are just warm. Do not let the eggs get too hot or they will scramble. Remove from the heat, place in the bowl of your mixer, and beat on high speed until they are tripled in volume, about 5–10 minutes. Fold eggs into chocolate until blended. Pour batter into prepared pan and smooth top. Cover pan loosely with greased foil.

4. Bake 15 minutes.

5. Cool cake, covered, on a rack for 30 minutes. Refrigerate at least 4 hours. Unmold onto a flat surface and invert onto a serving plate. Refrigerate until 45 minutes before serving. (The time is important because chocolate desserts are best when served at room temperature. This one is much less delicious when cold.) Cake will have fallen in the center. Spoon a thin layer of Raspberry Sauce into cavity on top of cake. Serve with whipped cream and remaining Raspberry Sauce. (This torte can be frozen provided it is well protected, first with plastic wrap and then with aluminum foil.)

Raspberry Sauce

Purée raspberries in the bowl of a food processor, fitted with the steel knife. (A blender may be used.) Strain to remove seeds. Stir sugar into puree and then add the Framboise or Kirsch. Blend well and refrigerate until ready to use.

1 10-ounce package frozen raspberries, thawed
3 tablespoons sugar
1 tablespoon Framboise or Kirsch (optional)

The epitome of flavor in a dessert is the combination of chocolate and raspberry. It is a heavenly marriage, and the resulting flavor is meant for the gods.

Doris Banchet's Italian Chocolate Torte

THE GRACIOUS LADY who is at the "front of the house" at Le Français Restaurant is an accomplished cook and baker in her own right. When I asked her to teach a class at a chocolate festival, she taught this recipe which she brought from Europe on a recent trip. It is a simple cake and is not too sweet.

6 ounces bittersweet
  chocolate
5 Grade A large eggs
8 ounces unsalted butter
  at room temperature
8 ounces sugar
1 5/16-ounce package
  vanilla sugar
8 ounces grated almonds
3 ounces all-purpose flour
1 teaspoon baking
  powder
1 cup whipping cream
Decor chips for garnish
  (optional)

Serves 12–14.

Bake this cake and keep it unfrosted in your freezer. Finish, as Doris suggests, or with any of the frostings, glazes, or mousses in this book. It can also be served plain with fruit or homemade ice cream.

1. Preheat oven to 350°F. Set aside a 10-inch spring-form pan.

2. Prep work: Grate chocolate fine and set aside. Separate eggs and set the bowls aside.

3. In a mixer bowl, mix the butter, sugar, vanilla sugar, and egg yolks until foamy. Add the almonds, chocolate, flour, and baking powder and mix well. Whip the egg whites until stiff but not dry and fold very carefully into the batter. Spoon mixture into the spring-form pan.

4. Bake 60–75 minutes.

5. Allow cake to cool in the pan on a rack. Remove the sides of the pan, invert the cake onto a serving plate, and very carefully remove the bottom of the pan. Whip the cream and frost the cake. Press decor chips onto the sides. Doris suggests an alternate frosting made by combining 6 ounces of powdered sugar with 3 tablespoons Meyer's Rum. (The cake layer freezes beautifully and you might want to keep several in your freezer. Be sure to wrap it well, first in plastic wrap and then in aluminum foil.)

Chocolate Marmalade Cake

THIS CAKE OFFERS AN **interesting combination of tastes. The layer is rich, made with two chocolates, and the topping has the tang of bitter orange marmalade.**

꙰

1. Preheat oven to 350°F. Butter an 8-inch round cake pan. Cut parchment paper to fit bottom and butter paper. Flour the lined pan and set aside.

2. Prep work: Chop the chocolate into small pieces and melt in the top of a double boiler over hot, not boiling, water. Stir until smooth, remove from heat, and cool to room temperature. Sift the flour, baking powder, and salt and set aside. Separate the eggs and set bowls aside.

3. In a mixer bowl, beat the butter until light and then gradually add sugar. Beat until light and fluffy. Add the yolks, one at a time, beating well after each addition. Stir in chocolate and ¼ cup of the marmalade. Gradually stir flour into batter until just blended. Stir in almonds. Beat whites until foamy, add the salt, and beat to stiff, not dry, peaks. Fold a third of the whites into batter to lighten it and then fold in the remaining whites in 2 additions. Pour batter into pan and smooth the top.

4. Bake 35 minutes or until a toothpick inserted in the center of the cake comes out clean.

5. Cool in pan 5 minutes; invert onto rack and cool completely. Heat remaining marmalade in a heavy saucepan over low heat, stirring constantly until thinned. Place cake on a serving plate. Brush remaining marmalade over cake in several thin layers, using a pastry brush. Let sit for 20 minutes at room temperature before serving. (The cake layer can be frozen plain, provided it is well wrapped, first in plastic wrap and then in aluminum foil.)

3 ounces semisweet chocolate
3 ounces unsweetened chocolate
1½ cups all-purpose flour
1 teaspoon baking powder
Pinch of salt
5 Grade A large eggs
¾ cup unsalted butter at room temperature
⅔ cup sugar
¾ cup bitter orange marmalade, divided
¼ cup ground almonds

Serves 8.

Susie's Flourless Chocolate Layer Cake

THIS CHOCOLATE LAYER CAKE is a scrumptious delight, filled and frosted with whipped cream and fresh strawberries. Wow! This Susie Skoog creation is great when the strawberries are large and delicious.

8 ounces semisweet
   chocolate
6 tablespoons water
8 Grade A large eggs
1 quart fresh strawberries
1½ cups sugar, divided
Pinch of salt
¼ teaspoon cream of
   tartar
3–4 cups whipping cream
½ teaspoon pure vanilla

Serves 8.

1. Preheat oven to 350°F. Butter 2 8-inch round cake pans. Cut parchment paper to fit the bottoms and butter the paper. Flour the lined pans and set aside.

2. Prep work: Chop the chocolate fine and place with water in the top of a double boiler over hot, not boiling, water. Stir until smooth, then remove from the heat and set aside. Separate the eggs and set the bowls aside. Wash, hull, and slice the strawberries, leaving 6–8 berries whole to garnish the top of the cake.

3. In a mixer bowl, beat the yolks, gradually adding 1 cup of the sugar. Beat until yolks are pale yellow and thick. Stir in the chocolate mixture. Beat whites until foamy; add salt and cream of tartar. Gradually increase the speed, beating until firm but not stiff. Fold a third of the whites into the chocolate mixture to lighten it. Fold in remaining whites. Divide batter between the two prepared pans and smooth the tops.

4. Bake 30–35 minutes or until a toothpick inserted in the middle comes out clean or reveals a dry crumb.

5. Cool the cake layers in their pans on a rack. Cakes will fall slightly while cooling. Meanwhile, whip the cream on low speed 5–10 minutes. As it starts to thicken, add the remaining ½ cup sugar and the vanilla. Beat at high speed until thick. Run a knife around the edge of the cake pans. Place a serving plate on the top of one of the layers and invert onto the plate. Remove the parchment paper. Spread with a thin layer of whipped cream and cover with sliced strawberries. Top the strawberries with another thin layer of whipped cream. Place the second cake layer on top and remove the parchment. Frost sides and top of the cake with remaining whipped cream. Decorate top of cake with whole berries. (The cake layers will freeze beautifully provided they are properly wrapped, first in plastic wrap and then in aluminum foil.)

Fresh or canned cherry halves, raspberries, blueberries, sliced nectarines, or sliced peaches can replace the strawberries in this recipe.

Perla Meyers' Chocolate Marquise with Pear Sauce

68

PERLA MEYERS has a marvelous sense of taste. Her recipes burst with flavor. The pear and chocolate in the recipe deliciously complement each other. Guests will be doubly delighted with this dessert.

⁂

¼ cup currants
1 cup water
¼ cup scotch whisky
6 ounces bittersweet
  chocolate
1 cup unsalted butter at
  room temperature
1 cup Dutch process
  cocoa, preferably
  Droste's
7 Grade A extra-large egg
  yolks
¾ cup sugar
1 cup whipping cream
1 cup additional
  whipping cream for
  garnish
Almond oil
Pear Sauce (recipe
  follows)

Serves 10–12.

1. Line the sides and bottom of a 1-quart narrow French porcelain terrine with a sheet of parchment paper, so that it extends 3 inches over each side. Lightly oil the paper and set aside. Perla recommends using almond oil as it is virtually tasteless and will not impart any flavor to the chocolate.

2. Prep work: In a small saucepan combine the currants and water. Place over high heat, bring to a simmer and immediately remove from the heat. Drain and pat dry on paper towels. In a small mixing bowl combine the plumped currants with the scotch whisky. Set aside to marinate for an hour. Break the chocolate into ½-inch pieces and place in the top of a double boiler over hot, not boiling, water. Stir until smooth and set aside to cool.

3. In the bowl of a food processor combine the butter and cocoa. Process until very smooth, stopping frequently to scrape down the sides of the bowl. In the bowl of a mixer combine the egg yolks and sugar. Beat until thick and pale yellow, about 3–5 minutes. Add melted chocolate to egg mixture and beat until well blended. Add the butter/cocoa mixture and beat until smooth. Stir in the marinated currants and scotch. In a separate bowl whip the cream and gently fold into the chocolate mixture. Pour into the prepared terrine. Smooth the top evenly with a spatula. Tap the terrine on the counter to eliminate air bubbles.

4. Cover terrine and refrigerate overnight. The next day, run a knife along each short side of the terrine. Invert the Marquise onto a rectangular platter. Carefully peel off the parchment. Garnish with rosettes of whipped cream.

5. To serve, allow Marquise to come to room temperature for 15 minutes. Cut the Marquise, with a knife dipped in hot water, crosswise into ½-inch slices. Place slices on individual serving plates. Spoon some of the pear sauce around each slice and serve immediately. (The Marquise can be frozen.)

Pear Sauce

1. Prep work: Peel the pears and place in acidulated water (water with lemon juice added to prevent discoloring) and set aside. Split the vanilla bean in half and set aside.

2. In a medium saucepan, combine the sugar and water. Add vanilla bean and bring to a boil. Add pears and reduce heat. Simmer, with saucepan partially covered for 18-20 minutes or until pears are tender when tested with the tip of a sharp knife. Remove from heat and allow pears to cool in the poaching liquid. Remove pears from liquid. Cut each in half lengthwise and remove the core. Set 2 halves aside. Cut remaining pears in half again and place in the bowl of a food processor together with ¼ cup of the poaching liquid and the Cointreau. Process until very smooth. Transfer to a small bowl and set aside. Dice the reserved pears into ¼-inch pieces. Fold into the pear puree. Taste and add more Cointreau if necessary.

3. Cover sauce and refrigerate until serving time.

*5 slightly underripe large
Bartlett or Bosc pears*
*1 3-inch piece vanilla
bean*
½ cup sugar
1½ cups water
*3-4 tablespoons
Cointreau*

Susie Skoog's Gianduja Cream Torte

GIANDUJA (pronounced john du yah) is the wonderful, sophisticated taste of milk chocolate and hazelnuts that is a European favorite. For a creative baker, like Susie, it took a short time in the kitchen to develop this delicious torte.

5 ounces Gianduja chocolate
4 tablespoons water
1/8 teaspoon cinnamon
4 Grade A large eggs
1/3 cup hazelnuts
6 tablespoons sugar, divided
1/4 cup potato starch
Pinch of salt
Gianduja Ganache (recipe follows)
Icing (recipe follows)

Serves 8.

1. Preheat oven to 350°F. Butter an 8-inch-by-3-inch round cake pan. Cut parchment paper to fit bottom and butter the paper. Flour the lined pan and set aside.

2. Prep work: Chop the Gianduja into small pieces and place in the top of a double boiler over hot, not boiling, water. Add water and cinnamon to the Gianduja and allow to melt. Stir until smooth and set aside to keep warm. Separate the eggs and set bowls aside. Place the hazelnuts on a baking sheet in a single layer and toast for 15 minutes. When nuts are evenly toasted, place in a clean dish towel and rub the skins off. Place in the bowl of a food processor fitted with the steel knife and grind until fine, using on/off turns. Set aside.

3. In a mixer bowl, beat the yolks and add 3 tablespoons of the sugar slowly. Beat to the ribbon stage. Stir in the hazelnuts and potato starch. Add the melted chocolate, stirring to combine. Beat the egg whites until foamy. Add a pinch of salt and beat until soft waves form. Slowly sprinkle on the remaining 3 tablespoons sugar and beat only until soft peaks form. Do not overbeat the whites! Gently fold whites into the chocolate mixture. Pour batter into the prepared pan and smooth the top.

4. Bake 30 minutes.

5. Cool cake on a rack. Turn the cooled cake onto an 8-inch cardboard round. Trim the sides and torte the cake to make 3 layers. Spread the bottom layer with half of the Gianduja Ganache. Place the second layer on top and spread with the remaining ganache. Top with the last cake layer and refrigerate until the cake is firm enough to decorate. Frost cake with two-thirds of the whipped

Gianduja Cream Icing. Place remaining icing in a pastry bag fitted with a star tip and pipe rosettes on top. (Curls made out of the Gianduja chocolate would be divine as decoration on top.) (The cake layers will freeze beautifully. Finish the cake on the day you are going to serve it. Be sure to wrap the layers well, first in plastic wrap and then in aluminum foil.)

Gianduja Ganache

1. Prep work: Chop the Gianduja chocolate into small pieces and set aside.

2. In a heavy saucepan, scald the cream (by bringing just to its boiling point). Add the Gianduja chocolate and whisk until smooth. Refrigerate ganache until firm enough to spread.

8 ounces Gianduja chocolate
½ cup whipping cream

Gianduja Cream Icing

Whip the cream on low speed of your mixer for 5-10 minutes. Raise the speed to medium and add the sugar and vanilla and whip until stiff.

3 cups heavy cream
¼ cup sugar
1 teaspoon vanilla

Perla Meyers' Chocolate Mousse Roulade

PERLA MEYERS is an expert at creating new tastes. Her recipes are prized possessions, made with ingredients that are in season. Chocolate is *always* in season, and this Roulade is always delicious.

⁂

2 ounces semisweet chocolate
1–2 tablespoons prepared espresso or strong coffee
6 Grade A large eggs
¾ cup sugar, divided
¼ cup unsweetened cocoa
Pinch of salt
Chocolate Mousse (recipe follows)
Powdered sugar to garnish

Serves 10–12.

1. Preheat oven to 375°F. Butter a 10-inch-by-15-inch jelly roll pan. Line the bottom and sides with a long strip of waxed paper; butter and flour the paper and set pan aside.

2. Prep work: Chop the chocolate into small pieces and melt in the espresso in the top of a double boiler over hot, not boiling, water. Remove from heat and cool slightly. Separate the eggs and set bowls aside.

3. In a mixer bowl, beat yolks until light and lemon-colored (4–5 minutes). Beat in half of the sugar at high speed, about 5 minutes or until very thick. Reduce speed; add chocolate mixture and cocoa; beat only until smooth. Beat the whites until frothy. Add salt and remaining sugar; beat to stiff, not dry, peaks. Mix a third of the whites into the chocolate mixture to lighten it, then carefully fold in the rest. Pour batter into pan and smooth top.

4. Bake 25–30 minutes or until cake springs back when touched lightly.

5. Wet and wring out a smooth kitchen towel. Run knife around the sides of the pan; spread towel over cake; top with another baking sheet and invert. Remove pan and carefully remove the waxed paper. Roll cake and towel together, starting at the long side. Place roll seam side down on rack to cool completely. Unroll roulade; spread with Chocolate Mousse; reroll roulade and place seam side down on a serving plate. Chill until serving time. Remove from refrigerator about 30 minutes before serving. Sprinkle with powdered sugar. Slice on an angle to give highly appetizing appearance. (Do not freeze this roulade.)

Chocolate Mousse

1. Chop the chocolate into small pieces and melt in the espresso in the top of a double boiler over hot, not boiling, water. Stir until smooth; remove from heat and allow to cool slightly. Cut butter into pieces and set aside.

2. Whisk butter pieces into chocolate and cool until mixture is like thick cream. Stir in yolks, one at a time, until well blended. Beat whites until foamy, add sugar, and beat to stiff, not dry, peaks. Mix a third of whites into chocolate mixture to lighten it, and carefully fold in the rest. Chill until thick but spreadable.

4 ounces bittersweet chocolate
2 tablespoons prepared espresso or strong coffee
1/3 cup unsalted butter at room temperature
2 Grade A large egg yolks
3 Grade A large egg whites
1 1/2 tablespoons sugar

Chocolate decorations may be purchased from gourmet shops, or from Madame Chocolate. Real chocolate vermicelli (called chocolate shot or sprinkles) are available in both fine and medium sizes. Decor chips—small, flat, shiny chips—are also available.

Barbara Grunes' Chocolate Flourless Cake

74

BARBARA GRUNES is the author of many cookbooks and dining guides. She has been a friend for longer than I would care to admit. This cake is appetizing when frosted and decorated with whipping cream.

6 ounces bittersweet
  chocolate
3 tablespoons prepared
  strong coffee
6 Grade A large eggs
⅔ cup plus 6 tablespoons
  sugar, divided
¼ teaspoon salt
1 cup whipping cream

Serves 10–12.

1. Preheat oven to 350°F. Butter a 9-inch springform pan and set aside.

2. Prep work: Chop chocolate into pieces and place in the coffee, in the top of a double boiler over hot, not boiling, water. Stir until smooth and set aside. Separate eggs and set bowls aside.

3. In a mixer bowl, beat the yolks with the ⅔ cup sugar on medium speed until thick and fluffy. Beat in melted chocolate, being sure the mixture is smooth. Beat whites until foamy. Add salt and continue to beat until firm, but not dry, peaks form. Mix a third of the whites into the chocolate mixture to lighten it, then carefully fold in remaining whites. Place a third of the batter into a small bowl; cover and refrigerate. Pour the remaining batter into prepared pan.

4. Bake 25 minutes, turn off oven, and leave cake in the oven for an additional 5 minutes. The center of the cake will fall, and a rim will form at the edges. The cake will be 1–1½ inches high.

5. While hot, remove springform sides and let the cake cool on a rack. Invert cake onto a plate, remove springform bottom and invert again onto a serving plate. When completely cooled, spread the refrigerated batter over the top of the cake and refrigerate for an additional hour. When ready to serve, slowly whip the cream until it begins to thicken. Sprinkle the remaining 6 tablespoons of sugar into the cream and beat until soft peaks form. Place the whipped cream into a pastry bag and decorate the top, using a star tip.

Alice Medrich's Bûche au Chocolat Chantilly

FROM COCOLAT BAKERY in Berkeley, California, and its proud owner, Alice Medrich, comes this recipe for a chocolate cake roll that is delicious just as it is as well as served with a raspberry or hot fudge sauce.

⚜

1. Preheat oven to 375°F. Butter an 11-inch-by-17-inch pan. Line with waxed paper that extends 2–3 inches over each end and butter the paper. Flour the lined pan and set aside.

2. Prep work: Chop chocolate into small pieces and place, along with the coffee and 1 teaspoon of the vanilla, in the top of a double boiler over hot, not boiling, water. Stir until smooth; remove from heat and cool slightly.

3. In a mixer bowl, beat the egg whites until foamy. Add salt and cream of tartar and beat to nearly firm peaks. Gradually add ½ cup of the sugar and beat to firm peaks. Fold a third of the meringue into the chocolate; then fold chocolate into remaining meringue. Pour mixture into prepared pan and smooth surface with a small spatula.

4. Bake 10 minutes, reduce heat to 350°F. and bake another 7 minutes.

5. Cool cake in pan. Turn pan over onto foil covered with an even layer of cocoa. Remove pan and peel off the paper. Whip cream until it begins to thicken; add 1½ teaspoons vanilla and 2–3 tablespoons sugar. Beat until nearly stiff. Spread cream (this cream mixture is called Chantilly) evenly onto cake and roll up, starting from the long side. Wrap roll in aluminum foil and refrigerate until serving time. To serve, decorate with sprigs of pine, fresh flowers, or holly at holiday time. Serve with Raspberry Sauce or Hot Fudge Sauce, if desired. (Do not freeze this cake.)

6 ounces semisweet chocolate
¼ cup prepared espresso or strong coffee, hot
2½ teaspoons pure vanilla, divided
5–6 Grade A large egg whites, enough to make ⅔ cup
Pinch of salt
½ teaspoon cream of tartar
½ cup plus 2–3 tablespoons sugar, divided
½ cup unsweetened Dutch process cocoa
1¼ cups whipping cream
Raspberry Sauce or Hot Fudge Sauce (see index)

Serves 12–15.

Chocolate Decadence

I CAME UPON this particular recipe during one of my early visits to California. Called by many names, claimed by many people, and even baked for sale by some, this recipe is undoubtedly a favorite of chocolate lovers. It is one of the richest cakes you'll ever eat, and you will enjoy every bite.

16 ounces bittersweet chocolate
10 tablespoons unsalted butter at room temperature
4 Grade A large eggs
1 tablespoon sugar
1 tablespoon flour
2 cups whipping cream
1 tablespoon powdered sugar
1 teaspoon pure vanilla
Chocolate curls for decoration
Raspberry Sauce (see index)

Serves 10–12.

This simple recipe is ideal for a chocolate cake tasting party. Ask each guest to bake this cake using a different brand or sweetness of chocolate. Sample each. The differences will be surprising.

1. Preheat oven to 425°F. Butter an 8-inch round cake pan. Cut parchment paper to fit the bottom and butter the paper. Flour the lined pan and set aside.

2. Prep work: Cut chocolate into small pieces. Place with butter in the top of a double boiler over hot, not boiling, water. Stir until smooth, remove from the heat and set aside.

3. In the top of another double boiler, whisk eggs and sugar over hot, not boiling, water. Whisk until sugar dissolves. The mixture will darken slightly and be barely warm to the touch. Remove from heat. Place the egg mixture in a mixer bowl and beat, at highest speed, until eggs are the consistency of light whipped cream. This will take about 5–10 minutes. Fold in the flour. Fold a third of egg mixture into the chocolate to lighten it. Add the rest of the egg mixture and fold in carefully, deflating the mixture as little as possible. Pour batter into pan and tap pan lightly on table to remove any air bubbles.

4. Bake 15 minutes. The center will be soft and the top will be crusty.

5. Cool on a rack. Cover the pan well with plastic wrap and freeze overnight. To serve, remove Decadence from the freezer early in the day. Turn onto a flat serving plate and remove the parchment paper. Whip the cream with the powdered sugar and vanilla until it forms soft peaks. Do not overwhip. Frost the cake, using two-thirds of the whipping cream. Top cake with chocolate curls.

Place the remaining whipped cream in a pastry bag, fitted with a star tip, and pipe rosettes around the edge of the cake. Top with a mountain of chocolate curls. Cut the cake into thin wedges and serve in a pool of Raspberry Sauce. (The Decadence layer freezes beautifully and can be made several weeks ahead of time, provided it is well wrapped, first with plastic wrap and then with aluminum foil.)

Chocolate curls can be made by warming a large chunk of chocolate (bittersweet, semisweet, or milk) with the heat from the bulb of a gooseneck lamp. Pull a long-bladed knife gently toward you and large curls will form. It may take a while to practice making perfect curls, but the best part is that you can eat your mistakes.

Bob Paroubek's Fudge Mousse Cake with St. Cecelia Sauce

THIS FUDGE MOUSSE CAKE is typical of the great desserts that Baker Bob has coming out of the kitchen of Toojay's. As a new Chicago restaurant, Toojay's is developing a reputation for its fine foods and desserts.

1½ cups cake flour
2 cups sugar
1 teaspoon baking powder
Pinch of salt
5 Grade A large eggs
½ cup milk
½ cup vegetable shortening
1 teaspoon pure vanilla
Fudge Mousse (recipe follows)
St. Cecelia Sauce (recipe follows)

Serves 8–10

1. Preheat oven to 350°F. Butter a 10-inch-by-15-inch jelly roll pan. Line with parchment paper, butter the paper, and set aside. Set aside a 9-inch-by-5-inch-by-3-inch loaf pan.

2. Prep work: Combine the cake flour, sugar, baking powder, and salt. Set aside.

3. In a mixer bowl, on medium speed, mix the eggs, milk, and shortening. Beat for 1 minute; slowly add the flour mixture to the bowl. Add the vanilla. Beat the batter for 10 minutes. Pour into the prepared jelly roll pan; spread evenly and smooth top.

4. Bake 15–20 minutes or until cake is firm to the touch and a toothpick inserted in the center comes out clean.

5. Cool cake in the pan on a rack. Turn out onto a piece of aluminum foil. Line the loaf pan with plastic wrap. Cut the cake to fit the bottom and sides of the pan. Cut another piece to fit the top and set aside. Pour in the Fudge Mousse. Cover mousse with the top piece. Refrigerate for several hours until the mousse becomes firm. Remove from loaf pan and cut into 1-inch slices. Lie slices flat on a plate and top with St. Cecelia Sauce. (The cake can be frozen, provided it is well protected, first with plastic wrap and then with aluminum foil. Do not freeze the Fudge Mousse or the St. Cecelia Sauce.)

Fudge Mousse

1. Prep work: Chop chocolate into small pieces and set aside. Separate eggs and set bowls aside.

2. In the top of a double boiler over hot, not boiling, water, melt the chocolate. Add vanilla, water, and sugar; stir until very smooth. Beat in the yolks, one at a time, being sure the mixture is smooth. Remove pan from heat. Beat the whites until foamy, adding the salt, and continue to beat until firm peaks form. Mix a third of the whites into the chocolate mixture to lighten it. Carefully fold in the remaining whites. Blend well.

24 ounces semisweet chocolate
9 Grade A large eggs
1 teaspoon pure vanilla
12 tablespoons water
3 heaping tablespoons powdered sugar
Pinch of salt

St. Cecelia Sauce

In a bowl beat the yolks; add salt and sugar, combining well. Beat in the cream and vanilla. Sauce will be thin. Refrigerate at least 1 hour before serving and serve chilled.

2 Grade A large egg yolks
⅛ teaspoon salt
1 cup powdered sugar
1 cup whipping cream
1 teaspoon pure vanilla

Bête Noire

LORA BRODY LIVES, SLEEPS, and eats chocolate. I was thrilled to receive her recipe from West Newton, Massachusetts. This cake will satisfy any chocoholic. It is delicious served warm or at room temperature; however, it is also good cold.

½ pound unsalted butter at room temperature
8 ounces unsweetened chocolate
4 ounces semisweet or bittersweet chocolate
½ cup water
1⅓ cups sugar, divided
5 Grade A extra-large eggs at room temperature
Whipped cream for garnish

Serves 8.

The flavor of chocolate is more intense when it is at room temperature. However, occasionally it is better cold. I think you'll like the flavor of the Bête Noir when it is cold. Try it both ways and see which way you like it best.

1. Preheat oven to 350°F. Place the rack in the center of the oven. Butter a 9-inch cake pan. Cut parchment paper to fit the bottom and butter the paper. Set pan aside. You will also need a slightly larger pan to use as a bain marie (water bath). Set aside.

2. Prep work: Cut butter into small pieces and set aside. Chop both chocolates into small pieces; set them aside. Place a teapot of water on to boil and keep hot.

3. In a heavy 1½-quart saucepan, combine the water with 1 cup of sugar. Bring to a rapid boil over high heat and cook for 2 minutes. Remove the pan from the heat and add the chocolate pieces immediately, stirring until they are completely melted. Add the butter, piece by piece, stirring to melt completely. In a mixer bowl, place the eggs and the remaining ⅓ cup sugar. For a cake with a crunchy crust, beat the eggs and sugar until they have tripled in volume; for a smooth top (better for frosting), mix the eggs and sugar only until the sugar dissolves. Add the chocolate mixture to the eggs and mix to incorporate completely. Do not overbeat! (This will cause air bubbles.) Spoon the mixture into the prepared pan. Set the pan into the larger pan and set both pans in the oven. Pour hot water into the larger pan to form the bain marie.

4. Bake for 20–25 minutes.

5. Let cool in the pan for 10 minutes and then run a sharp knife around the sides to release the cake. Cover with plastic wrap and unmold onto a baking sheet. Invert a serving plate over the cake and flip it over so the plate is on the bottom and the cake on top. Serve warm or at room temperature, garnished with unsweetened whipped cream.

Chocolate Pound Cake

BARBARA GRUNES IS INTO **many facets of the food world. As busy as she may be, she loves to cook and bake for her husband, Jerry, and youngest daughter, Dorothy. They love this cake topped with homemade ice cream and hot fudge sauce.**

1. Preheat oven to 325°F. Grease the bottom of an 8-inch-by-4-inch loaf pan. Line the pan with parchment paper and set aside.

2. Prep work: Sift the flour, cocoa, baking soda, baking powder, and salt; set aside.

3. In a mixer bowl, beat the butter and sugar until light and fluffy. Add the eggs, one at a time, beating well after each addition. Stir in the sour cream and then the flour mixture. Add the vanilla and chocolate extracts and mix well. Pour into the prepared pan. Smooth the top.

4. Bake 75 minutes or until a toothpick inserted in the middle comes out clean.

5. Allow cake to cool in the pan. While cooling, prick several times with the tines of a fork. Sprinkle with crème de cacao. Remove from pan onto a serving plate. Sprinkle with powdered sugar at the last moment before serving. (The cake can be frozen, provided it is well protected, first with plastic wrap and then with aluminum foil.)

1³⁄₄ cups all-purpose flour
¹⁄₂ cup cocoa
1¹⁄₂ teaspoons baking soda
1 teaspoon baking powder
1 teaspoon salt
6 tablespoons unsalted butter at room temperature
1¹⁄₄ cups sugar
3 Grade A large eggs
1 cup sour cream
1 teaspoon pure vanilla
1 teaspoon chocolate extract
2 tablespoons crème de cacao liqueur, or to taste
Powdered sugar

Serves 8–10.

Slice this pound cake horizontally and fill with whipped cream and fruit. Slice it vertically and use as a "shortcake" to serve with fresh fruit.

Chocolate Overdose

THIS RECIPE has been published in many variations and called by many names. Its taste is a suitable reward for the time and effort required to make it. The cake is quite rich and it should be served in very thin slices.

½ *cup almonds*
1 recipe Meringue Layer (recipe follows)
1 recipe Chocolate Ganache (recipe follows)
1 recipe Chocolate Genoise (recipe follows)
Crème de cacao
1 recipe Mousse au Chocolat (recipe follows)
2-3 cups whipping cream

Serves 16.

1. Place almonds in a single layer on a baking sheet and place in a 350°F. oven for 15 minutes. Shake pan to toast evenly. Cool nuts and chop in your food processor. Set aside.

2. With the meringue layer back in its original pan, spoon all the ganache over it in a smooth, even layer. Place one of the genoise layers on top of the ganache. Sprinkle each genoise layer with crème de cacao as you set it in place. Place in freezer to chill before continuing. Cover genoise with half of the mousse. Top with second layer of genoise and then the remaining mousse. Top with remaining layer of genoise. Cover with plastic wrap and chill for 4-6 hours. Whip the cream to stiff peaks. Remove the springform sides carefully. When the cake is cold, remove the bottom of the pan and the parchment paper. Frost the cake with the whipped cream and cover the sides with the toasted almonds. Refrigerate until serving time.

All the components of this cake can be made a day or two in advance. The genoise can be frozen, if properly protected, first in plastic wrap and then in aluminum foil. The meringue should be kept in a tin to stay crispy. The ganache and mousse must be refrigerated. Do not freeze the finished cake.

Pictured on color plate 3.

Meringue Layer

1. Preheat oven to 350°F. Line the bottom of a 10-inch springform pan with parchment paper. Butter the paper and the sides of the pan. Set aside.

2. Prep work: Place the almonds in a single layer on a baking sheet and place in the oven for 15 minutes. (The almonds used to decorate the sides of the finshed cake may be toasted at the same time.) Cool nuts and grind to a fine powder in your food processor. Set aside.

3. Turn oven down to 250°F. Combine the whites and the sugar in the top of a double boiler. Heat to lukewarm, stirring constantly to dissolve sugar. Remove from heat and pour into mixer bowl. Beat about 15 minutes at medium speed until stiff. Quickly fold in cocoa and the almonds. Place this meringue in a pastry bag fitted with a plain round tube. Pipe, forming a spiral effect on the bottom of the springform pan. Start from the center and work outward until completely covered.

4. Bake for 2–2½ hours or until brittle and very light.

5. Cool meringue in pan. Remove the side of the pan and take the layer out very carefully, allowing parchment paper to remain. Place layer back in pan and set aside.

⅓ cup almonds
3 Grade A large egg
*   whites*
⅓ cup sugar
2 tablespoons
*   unsweetened cocoa*

Chocolate Ganache

Chop the chocolate into small pieces and heat with the whipping cream in the top of a double boiler over simmering water until chocolate melts. Stir until smooth. Cool to room temperature. Beat for a few minutes to blend. If refrigerated allow it to return to room temperature and beat before using.

8 ounces bittersweet
*   chocolate*
1 cup whipping cream

Chocolate Genoise

10 Grade A large eggs
1 tablespoon unsalted
   butter at room
   temperature
¾ cup sugar
1½ cups cake flour
2 tablespoons
   unsweetened cocoa

1. Preheat oven to 350°F. Butter a 10-inch-by-3-inch round cake pan. Cut parchment paper to fit the bottom and butter the paper. Set aside.

2. Prep work: Beat the eggs lightly and set aside. Melt the butter and set aside.

3. Combine the eggs and sugar in the top of a double boiler. Heat to lukewarm, stirring constantly, to dissolve the sugar. Remove from heat. Pour the mixture into a mixer bowl and beat on high speed for about 5–10 minutes or until the batter forms a ribbon. Sift the flour and cocoa into the batter and fold in. Fold in the melted butter. Pour into the prepared pan and smooth top.

4. Bake 30 minutes or until cake springs back when touched lightly. A toothpick inserted in the center should come out clean.

5. Cool cake in the pan. Remove from pan and torte into three layers, trimming off top and bottom crust with a sharp serrated knife. Set aside.

Mousse au Chocolat

1 pound bittersweet
   chocolate
8 tablespoons water
8 Grade A large egg
   whites
½ cup sugar
6 Grade A large egg yolks

Chop the chocolate into small pieces and heat with the water in the top of a double boiler over simmering water until melted. Stir until completely smooth and remove from heat. Beat whites until soft peaks form. Gradually beat sugar into the whites and continue beating until stiff peaks form. Beat yolks into the chocolate mixture one at a time. Lightly fold a third of the egg whites into the chocolate mixture to lighten it. Fold in remaining whites and chill.

Chocolate Fudge Cake à la Susie

SUSIE SKOOG'S CAKES **are delicious and this one is especially easy to bake. Top it off with powdered sugar or any of the frostings and sauces from my book.**

꘎

1. Preheat oven to 350°F. Butter a 9-inch cake pan. Cut parchment paper to fit the bottom and butter the paper. Flour the lined pan and set aside.

2. Prep work: Cut chocolate into small pieces and place in the top of a double boiler over hot, not boiling, water. Stir until smooth and set aside.

3. In a large mixing bowl, using a whisk, beat the butter into melted chocolate. Beat in sugar and then the eggs, one at a time. Beat until mixture lightens slightly in color. Beat in flour just until it disappears. Pour batter into prepared pan and smooth the top.

4. Bake 25 minutes or until a toothpick inserted 1 inch from the outside of the pan reveals a dry crumb.

5. Cool in the pan on a rack. Invert cake onto a serving plate and remove parchment paper. Dust with powdered sugar to garnish. (This cake freezes beautifully, provided it is well wrapped, first with plastic wrap and then with aluminum foil. Several may be made and kept in the freezer for unexpected company.)

6 ounces semisweet chocolate
½ cup unsalted butter at room temperature
⅔ cup sugar
3 Grade A large eggs
½ cup cake flour
Powdered sugar for garnish

Serves 8.

This cake can be served in a pool of Crème Anglaise or Raspberry Sauce (see Index), with a scoop of mousse or ice cream. The cake can be frosted or glazed, as desired.

10

Cheesecakes

Cheesecakes are sensuous, smooth, creamy, and delicious. The addition of chocolate produces a heavenly dessert. Cream cheese cakes are totally American and are our contribution to the world's cheesecakes.

The recipes included in this chapter are wonderful—you'll love all of them. Feel free to substitute one sweetness or brand of chocolate for another. The differences in taste will provide pleasant surprises. Experiment with chocolate—you won't be sorry.

Tips for Baking

- Experiment with the crust. Vanilla wafers and tea biscuits make delicious crusts. Use your imagination.
- Beat the cream cheese for a long time until it is completely smooth. Then and only then add the rest of the ingredients.
- The center of a cheesecake may be a bit soft when the recipe says it's done. Cheesecakes firm up as they cool.
- A cracked cheesecake is usually caused by too high an oven temperature or too long a baking period. Do not be upset if this happens—the topping covers all problems.
- Cheesecakes are delicious the next day, but they must be refrigerated.
- These cheesecakes will all freeze beautifully.

Jolene Worthington's Chocolate Velvet Cheesecake

THIS CHEESECAKE, which has a fine texture, was created by Jolene Worthington. She is a wonderful baker, food writer, and food stylist. This cake is rich and creamy, but not heavy—a cake for a true chocoholic.

1 8½-ounce package chocolate wafer cookies

⅓ cup plus 2 tablespoons unsalted butter at room temperature

12 ounces semisweet chocolate

Pinch of salt

Pinch of cinnamon

2 8-ounce packages cream cheese at room temperature

⅔ cup sugar

1½ cups heavy cream, sour cream, or a combination of both

1 teaspoon pure vanilla

3 Grade A large eggs

Decorations for top of cake: ⅓ cup Dutch process cocoa, whipped cream, chocolate shavings or curls (optional)

Serves 12–14.

1. Preheat oven to 350°F. Open a 9-inch springform pan and remove the bottom. Cover the bottom with a larger piece of aluminum foil, smoothing the top and tucking the excess under. Flatten the underside of the foil so the bottom will sit level. Place it back into the pan and tighten the spring. (This is a trick taught to me by Maida Heatter. It will always help you take the cake out of the pan and off the bottom easily.)

2. Prep work: Crush the chocolate wafer cookies into crumbs and set aside. Melt butter and set aside. Chop the chocolate into small pieces and melt in the top of a double boiler over hot, not boiling, water; stir until smooth; remove from heat and set aside.

3. In a small bowl, combine the cookie crumbs, salt, cinnamon, and ⅓ cup of the melted butter. Press the mixture firmly onto the bottom and sides (three-fourths of the way up) of the springform pan. Chill 30 minutes. Meanwhile, in a mixer bowl, beat the cream cheese until smooth. Add sugar and beat until smooth. Scrape the sides of the bowl frequently. Add heavy cream, the remaining 2 tablespoons butter, and vanilla. Beat until smooth. Add eggs, one at a time, incorporating one before adding another. Be sure the batter is smooth and then mix in the melted chocolate. Combine well. Pour the batter into the chilled crust.

4. Bake 15 minutes at 350°F., then reduce the heat to 325°F. for an additional 45 minutes.

5. Cool in the pan on a baking rack. Refrigerate overnight. When ready to serve cheesecake, remove sides of pan. Lift the cake off bottom with the aluminum foil. Carefully loosen the foil with your hands. Use a large spatula to place the cheesecake on your serving plate. Place cocoa in a small, fine mesh strainer and dust top of cake. Decorate top with whipped cream, chocolate shavings or curls, or leave plain as desired. (This cake will freeze beautifully. Protect first with plastic wrap and then with aluminum foil.)

Pictured on color plate 4.

Many years ago, during cooking classes in California, James Beard gave me his recipe for making vanilla. Slit 4 or 5 vanilla beans and let them marinate for two weeks in a pint of fine cognac.

Gianduja Cheesecake

NANCY HARRIS BECAME addicted to
Gianduja—a combination of milk chocolate and
hazelnuts—when our first shipment arrived from
Switzerland. Nancy developed this recipe for the Hyatt
Chocolate Fest. Now she bakes this cake for her
catering clients.

2 cups hazelnuts
12 ounces Gianduja
  chocolate
3 tablespoons unsalted
  butter at room
  temperature
½ cup plus 2 tablespoons
  sugar, divided
24 ounces cream cheese at
  room temperature
2 Grade A large eggs
⅓ cup Frangelico liqueur
¾ cup whipping cream
Whipped cream to
  decorate top of cake
  (optional)

Serves 10–12.

1. Preheat the oven to 350°F. Open a 9-inch spring-form pan and remove the bottom. Cover the bottom with a larger piece of aluminum foil, smoothing the top and tucking the excess under. Flatten the underside of the foil so the bottom will sit level. Place the bottom back into the pan and tighten the spring. (The foil is Maida Heatter's trick.) Spray the pan with Pam and set aside.

2. Prep work: Place the hazelnuts on a baking sheet in a single layer and toast in a 350°F. oven for 15 minutes. When evenly toasted, place in a clean dish towel and rub the skins off. Set aside. Increase oven temperature to 400°F. for a later step. Chop the Gianduja chocolate into small pieces and put in the top of a double boiler and allow to melt over hot, not boiling, water. Set aside.

3. Place the nuts, butter, and 2 tablespoons of the sugar in the bowl of a food processor fitted with a steel knife. Process, using on/off turns, until the nuts are chopped and the mixture is well blended. Spread over the bottom and halfway up the sides of the prepared pan. Bake at 400°F. for 6 minutes. Set aside and allow to cool. Turn oven down to 350°F. Meanwhile, prepare the filling. Place the cream cheese in the bowl of a food processor fitted with a steel knife. (A mixer may be used instead.) Process until well blended. Add the remaining ingredients in the following order, processing each ingredient until well blended: the remaining sugar, eggs, Gianduja chocolate, Frangelico, and finally the cream. Pour into cooled crust.

4. Bake cheesecake for 1 hour.

5. Remove from oven and allow to cool. Refrigerate for at least 6 hours or preferably overnight. If desired, frost top with whipped cream topped with rosettes. (This cheesecake freezes beautifully. Protect first with plastic wrap and then with aluminum foil.)

Frangelico liqueur combines the flavors of hazelnuts and berries. It is a wonderful addition to a recipe containing hazelnuts.

Marble Cheesecake

THIS IS A VARIATION of a recipe that appeared in *The New York Times* many years ago. It is a Craig Claiborne recipe with a chocolate touch. This luscious recipe has been adapted for the food processor so it can be made very quickly.

※

4 ounces bittersweet
  chocolate
4 8-ounce packages cream
  cheese at room
  temperature
1½ cups sugar
1 teaspoon pure vanilla
¼ teaspoon almond
  extract
4 Grade A large eggs
⅓ cup graham cracker
  crumbs
Chocolate curls for
  decoration (optional)

Serves 10–12.

1. Preheat oven to 350°F. Butter an 8-inch-round-by-3-inch-deep seamless cheesecake pan. Cut parchment paper to fit the bottom and butter the lined pan. Do not use a springform pan! Set aside a 9-inch-by-13-inch pan to use as a bain marie (water bath) when baking the cheesecake.

2. Prep work: Chop the chocolate into small pieces and melt in the top of a double boiler over hot, not boiling, water until smooth. Remove pan from heat and set aside. Fill a teapot with water and bring to a boil and keep hot.

3. Place cream cheese in the bowl of a food processor fitted with the steel blade. Process cream cheese until it is very smooth. Stop the machine several times to scrape down the sides of the bowl. Add the sugar, vanilla, and almond extract and process until well blended. Add the eggs through the feed tube, one at a time, processing until smooth between additions. Remove a third of the batter and add to the melted chocolate. Mix together until smooth. Place alternating large spoonfuls of white batter and small spoonfuls of chocolate batter into the prepared pan. Place filled pan in the larger pan and add water to cover two-thirds of cheesecake pan.

4. Bake 90 minutes.

5. Remove pan from water bath and cool on a rack. When cake is completely cool, invert onto a serving plate. (I find it helpful to sprinkle the plate with powdered sugar so the cheesecake will not stick.) Remove the parchment paper. Sprinkle the bottom of the cake with the graham cracker crumbs, pat lightly so they will stick, and invert the cake onto the plate you wish to serve it on. Chill for 5–6 hours or overnight. Before serving, garnish top of cake with chocolate curls. (Cheesecake can be refrigerated several days. It freezes beautifully if well protected, first with plastic wrap and then with aluminum foil.)

Bittersweet chocolate and semisweet chocolate may be interchanged to create interesting flavor variations.

Chocolate Almond-Swirl Cheesecake

Susie Skoog Created this cake for a special friend. Her friend was delighted with the first taste. It has become a special favorite.

⎯⎯ ⚜ ⎯⎯

1 cup almonds
4 ounces semisweet
chocolate
4 8-ounce packages cream
cheese at room
temperature
1½ cups sugar
1 cup heavy cream
½ cup sour cream
¼ teaspoon almond
extract
4 Grade A large eggs
Chocolate curls for
decoration (optional)

Serves 10–12.

1. Preheat oven to 300°F. Butter bottom and sides of an 8-inch-round-by-3-inch-deep seamless cheesecake pan. Do not use a springform pan! Cut a parchment paper circle to fit the bottom of the pan. Butter the paper. Set aside a 9-inch-by-13-inch pan to use as a bain marie (water bath) when baking the cheesecake.

2. Prep work: Place the almonds on a baking sheet and toast in the oven about 15 minutes until lightly browned. When cool, chop them in a food processor fitted with a steel knife and set aside. Chop the chocolate into small pieces and melt in the top of a double boiler over hot, not boiling, water, until smooth. Remove pan from heat and set aside. Fill a teapot with water, bring to the boil, and keep hot.

3. In a mixer bowl, beat the cream cheese on high speed to lighten. Add sugar, heavy cream, sour cream, and almond extract. Beat until smooth. Stop the mixer frequently to scrape down the sides of the bowl. Reduce speed to low and add eggs, one at a time. Beat just enough to incorporate the eggs. Do not overbeat! Place half of the batter in a separate bowl and stir in the melted chocolate. Blend until smooth. Stir the almonds into the remaining white batter. Alternate layers of chocolate and almond batter in the prepared pan. Use the tip of a knife to swirl the batter slightly. Place the cheesecake pan in the larger pan and add 1 inch of hot water.

4. Bake for 2 hours, turn off the oven, and leave cheesecake in the oven for 1 hour more.

5. Cool the cheesecake for several hours. Invert pan onto serving plate; remove the pan and the parchment paper. Cover top of cake with chocolate curls if desired. (This cheesecake can be refrigerated for several days. The cake freezes beautifully if you wrap it well, first in plastic wrap and then in aluminum foil.)

Almonds and chocolate are a very special flavor combination. These two are also paired in Luscious Chocolate Almond Sauce and Jackie Etcheber's Banana Tart with Chocolate Sauce.

11

Pies and Pastries

These recipes are the most delicious, decadent pies you've ever tasted. Each is worth the time it takes to make it because each bite of each pie is an outstanding experience. Experiment with different chocolates, exchanging one chocolate for another.

Tips for Baking Pies

A chocolate crust is included at the end of this chapter. A recipe for plain pie crust is not included here because recipes are available in cookbooks like *The Fannie Farmer Cookbook* or *The Art of Food Processor Cooking*.

- Use a glass pie plate and be sure your crust is golden brown.
- Crusts can be baked at any time; in fact, you can make several and freeze them. (Be sure to wrap them well so they don't dry out.)
- Make the filling early on the day you are going to serve the pie so the filling will chill until firm before topping is added to the pie.
- If you paint the inside of the empty baked shell with a very thin layer of melted chocolate and allow the chocolate to set, you can fill the crust a day in advance and it will not get soggy.
- The Orange Lait Chocolate has a unique taste that will broaden one's baking repertoire.

Chocolate Cream Pie

CHOCOLATE CREAM PIE is gaining in popularity. Delicious recipes, such as this, account for the change in America's taste.

1 fully baked 9-inch pie crust
3 ounces unsweetened chocolate
3 Grade A large egg yolks
1 cup plus 2 tablespoons sugar
3 tablespoons cornstarch
½ teaspoon salt
3 cups milk
4 tablespoons unsalted butter at room temperature
1½ teaspoons pure vanilla
Topping (recipe follows)
Semisweet chocolate, shaved for garnish

Serves 8–10.

1. A 9-inch pie crust, baked and ready to be filled, is needed for this recipe.

2. Prep work: Chop the chocolate fine and set aside. Lightly beat the yolks and set aside.

3. In a heavy saucepan, mix the sugar, cornstarch, and salt. Stir in the milk and then add the chocolate. Cook over medium-high heat, stirring constantly, until mixture comes to a boil. Reduce heat and cook 1 minute more. Remove from heat. Stir the mixture so that it is very smooth. Add a third of the hot mixture to the egg yolks to warm them, then quickly stir the yolks back into the saucepan. Stir in the butter and vanilla. Remove from heat and stir occasionally as mixture cools. Pour into the prepared pie crust.

4. Cover the pie and allow it to chill at least 3 hours. Spread topping over chilled filling and garnish with shaved chocolate. Chill another hour.

Topping

1 cup heavy cream
2 tablespoons sugar
¼ teaspoon pure vanilla

Beat cream on low speed until slightly thickened. Add sugar and vanilla; increase speed and beat until almost stiff.

Susie Skoog's Valrhôna Orange Pie

THIS PIE WAS INSPIRED BY the arrival of a new French chocolate—a combination of milk chocolate and mandarin orange. When Susie first tasted the Orange Lait chocolate she couldn't wait to create a new recipe to take advantage of this wonderful taste.

1. A 9-inch pie crust, baked and ready to be filled, is needed for this recipe.

2. Prep work: Chop the chocolate into small pieces and melt with the coffee in the top of a double boiler over hot, not boiling, water. Stir until smooth; remove from heat and set aside. Separate eggs and set bowls aside.

3. With a whisk, stir the butter into the chocolate mixture, a tablespoon at a time, until all is incorporated. Add the egg yolks and blend well. Beat the whites until foamy; add the salt; continue to beat and slowly add the sugar until the whites become stiff but not dry. Mix a third of the whites into the chocolate mixture to lighten it and carefully fold in the rest. Pour into the prepared pie shell.

4. Cover pie and allow it to chill for at least 3 hours. Spread topping over chilled filling.

1 fully baked 9-inch pie crust
6 ounces Valrhôna Orange Lait chocolate
2 tablespoons brewed strong coffee
3 Grade A large eggs
6 tablespoons unsalted butter at room temperature
Pinch of salt
¼ cup sugar
Topping (recipe follows)

Serves 8.

Topping

Beat the cream on low speed until slightly thickened. Add the sugar and vanilla; increase the speed and beat until almost stiff.

1 cup whipping cream
¼ cup sugar
1 teaspoon pure vanilla

Pictured on color plate 5.

Café Cream Pie

THE NESTLÉ COMPANY has a fine kitchen staff developing recipes. They are justifiably proud of this recipe which they provided for this book. Nestlé sells more than 240 million Toll House Semisweet real chocolate morsels each day—which would make a lot of these pies!

1½ cups nuts
6 ounces Nestlé Toll
  House semisweet
  chocolate morsels
1 tablespoon vegetable
  shortening
Café Cream Filling
  (recipe follows)
Chocolate curls for
  garnish

Serves 8.

1. Line a 9-inch pie pan, smoothly, with aluminum foil and set aside.

2. Prep work: Chop the nuts fine and set aside.

3. In the top of a double boiler over hot, not boiling, water, combine the chocolate morsels and shortening. Stir until morsels are melted and smooth. Add chopped nuts and mix well. Spread evenly on bottom and up sides (not over rim) of prepared pie pan.

4. Chill in refrigerator until firm, about 1 hour. Lift chocolate shell out of the pan; remove foil and place shell back into pie pan or onto serving plate. Pour filling into shell; chill in refrigerator until firm, about 1 hour. Garnish with chocolate curls. (Choco-nut crust can be made in advance if it is well protected, first with plastic wrap and then with aluminum foil. It should be kept in a cool, dark, dry place away from odors.)

Café Cream Filling

½ pound marshmallows
  (about 40 large)
⅓ cup milk
¼ teaspoon salt
3 tablespoons coffee-
  flavored liqueur
3 tablespoons vodka
1½ cups whipping cream

In the top of a double boiler over hot, not boiling, water, combine the marshmallows, milk, and salt. Heat until the marshmallows melt. Stir until smooth and remove from heat. Add the liquors; stir well until blended. (The coffee-flavored liqueur and vodka can be reduced to 2 tablespoons each.) Transfer to a small bowl and chill until slightly thickened (45–60 minutes), stirring occasionally. Remove from refrigerator and whisk thickened filling until smooth. Whip the cream to almost stiff peaks. Gently fold into filling. Use to fill pie shell.

Ricotta Cheese Chocolate Chip Pie

THIS IS A DELICIOUSLY DIFFERENT **kind of chocolate pie. It is neither too sweet nor too rich.**

1. Preheat oven to 350°F. A 9-inch deep dish pie pan will be needed.

2. Prep work: Place the almonds on a baking sheet in a single layer and toast for 15 minutes or until evenly browned. Chop 1 cup and set them aside. Set aside the remaining ¼ cup. Melt the butter and set aside.

3. Make the crust: Mix the graham cracker crumbs, superfine sugar, and melted butter. Press evenly and firmly against the bottom and sides of the pie pan. Bake 10–12 minutes and then cool completely. In a mixer bowl, beat the ricotta cheese and ¾ cup sugar. When well blended, stir in the chopped almonds and the chips. Beat 1 cup of the cream and the almond extract to soft peaks. Fold into the cheese mixture. Do not overfold. Pour into the cooled crust.

4. Allow the pie to chill for several hours or overnight. Before serving, whip the remaining 1 cup of cream with the remaining ¼ cup sugar to firm peaks. Decorate the top of the pie with the whipped cream and sprinkle with the ¼ cup toasted sliced almonds.

1¼ cups sliced almonds, divided

6 tablespoons unsalted butter at room temperature

1¼ cups graham cracker crumbs

¼ cup superfine sugar

1¼ pounds dry ricotta cheese (drain if necessary)

1 cup sugar, divided

½ cup semisweet chocolate mini chips

2 cups whipping cream, divided

½ teaspoon almond extract

Serves 8–10.

Be selective with the pie crust recipes you use. In keeping with the flavor of this book, you will want to try Jolene Worthington's Chocolate Pie Crust.

Chocolate Pecan Pie

THIS PIE IS WONDERFUL for family dinners and picnics. It travels well. It is loaded with pecans and chocolate chips.

1 partially baked 9-inch pie crust (baked ¾ of the way)
1½ cup pecans
¼ cup unsalted butter at room temperature
6 ounces semisweet chocolate chips
½ cup light corn syrup
½ cup sugar
2 Grade A extra-large eggs
Unsweetened whipped cream for garnish

Serves 8.

This is a special pie because it is a chocolate pecan pie. The chocolate chips sprinkled on the crust add wonderful flavor. The flavor can be varied by substituting bittersweet or milk chocolate chips for the semisweet ones.

1. Preheat the oven to 325°F. You will need a 9-inch pie crust, three-fourths baked and ready to be filled.

2. Prep work: Chop the pecans coarsely and set aside. Melt butter and set aside to cool.

3. Sprinkle the nuts and chips evenly in the crust. In a mixer bowl, blend the corn syrup, sugar, and eggs. Add the melted butter and mix until well blended. Pour slowly (so as not to disturb the nuts and chips) into the crust.

4. Bake 45–60 minutes.

5. Place pie on a rack. Serve warm, or at room temperature, with a dollop of the unsweetened whipped cream.

Jolene Worthington's Chocolate Pie Crust

103

CHOCOLATE LOVERS are especially pleased with this chocolate crust. Jolene's creation will make a chocolate pie doubly delicious and will enhance the taste of any fruit or cream pie.

🔆

1. Preheat oven to 450°F. Set aside a 9-inch pie plate or a 10-inch tart pan with a removable bottom.

2. Prep work: Chop chocolate into small pieces and melt in the top of a double boiler over hot, not boiling, water. Remove from the heat and allow to cool to room temperature. Cut the butter into ½-inch cubes.

3. Place the flour in a medium-sized bowl and cut in the butter with a pastry cutter until the mixture resembles coarse crumbs. Dissolve the salt in the water and stir into the chocolate. Add the chocolate mixture to the flour mixture tossing with a fork until the mixture holds its shape. Remove dough from bowl and knead several times. Form into a ball, flatten, cover with plastic wrap and refrigerate two hours. After refrigerating, tap dough lightly to soften. Roll on a lightly floured surface into a 12-inch circle. (Dough can also be rolled between two pieces of wax or parchment paper.) Work quickly while dough is still cold. When the circle is formed, wrap dough around the rolling pin and place over the tart pan or pie plate. Ease into pan, with fingertip pressure against bottom and sides. Using a knife, trim the dough even with the edge of the pan. Refrigerate 15 minutes. Prick bottom and sides with a fork.

4. Bake on the bottom rack of your oven about 10 minutes until pastry edges are crisp. Lower oven to 300°F. and bake an additional 10 minutes until pastry is crisp.

5. Cool in pan on a rack.

6. This crust can be frozen, empty, provided it is well protected, first with plastic wrap and then with aluminum foil.

3 ounces bittersweet chocolate
½ cup unsalted butter
1⅓ cups all-purpose flour
Pinch salt
2 tablespoons warm water

Makes 1 9-inch pie crust.

Jackie Etcheber's Banana Tart with Chocolate Sauce

JACKIE ETCHEBER is the owner/chef of an excellent Chicago restaurant. She gained her experience in the kitchens of La Mer and The Ritz Carlton Hotel. Her restaurant is acclaimed for its delicious chocolate desserts. This is a sophisticated, adult version of chocolate-covered bananas from our childhood.

1 cup almonds
Apricot preserves
1½ cups unsalted butter at room temperature
½ cup sugar
2 cups all-purpose flour
Pinch of salt
2 Grade A large eggs
3 large bananas
Pastry Cream (recipe follows)
Jackie's Chocolate Sauce (recipe follows)

Serves 10.

This is a basic tart recipe. Any fresh, canned, or cooked fruit (berries, peaches, apricots, or nectarines) can be used in place of the bananas. Walnuts, pecans, or hazelnuts may replace the almonds in the crust.

1. Preheat the oven to 350°F. Set aside a 10-inch quiche/tart pan. Have some aluminum pie pellets on hand for weighing down the tart shell during baking. Dried beans or rice can be substituted.

2. Prep work: Toast the almonds in a single layer for 15 minutes until they are evenly browned. In the bowl of a food processor fitted with the steel blade, process the almonds until they are powdered and set aside. Heat the preserves, strain them, and set the liquid aside.

3. Make the dough: In a mixer bowl fitted with a dough hook, cream butter and sugar until light and fluffy; add almonds and beat well. Add flour, salt, and eggs and knead, with the dough hook, until dough is smooth and shiny. Refrigerate dough 4 hours or overnight. (The dough may be frozen, provided it is well protected, first with plastic wrap and then with aluminum foil.) On a lightly floured surface, roll the dough into a 12-inch circle. Fold the dough in half and place carefully over half the pan. Open the folded dough and fit into pan using fingertip pressure. Roll a rolling pin across the rim of the pan to remove excess dough. Cover the top of the dough with a piece of aluminum foil, shiny side down (if the shiny side is up, the heat is reflected away). Fit foil to the dough. Fill with pie pellets.

4. Bake for 25 minutes or until lightly browned, removing aluminum foil and pie pellets after the first 15 minutes.

5. Allow shell to cool. Fill three-fourths full with Pastry Cream. Top with sliced bananas placed in overlapping circles covering the entire top. Paint lightly with apricot preserves. Chill until ready to serve. Slice into wedges and serve in a pool of Jackie's Chocolate Sauce. (The shell may be frozen, provided it is well protected, first with plastic wrap and then with aluminum foil. The finished tart should not be frozen.)

Pastry Cream

1. Prep work: In a heavy saucepan over medium heat, bring the milk and vanilla just to a boil. Remove from heat and set aside.

2. In a mixer bowl, combine the yolks and the sugar and beat to the ribbon stage. Add flour and blend well. Add half of the milk very slowly to the egg mixture to warm it. (Do not add too fast or the yolks will cook.) Return mixture to the saucepan and cook over low heat, stirring constantly, until mixture thickens. Strain and cool. (Pastry Cream can be made several days in advance and stored in a tightly covered container in the refrigerator. Place a piece of plastic wrap directly on the cream so a skin won't form.)

2 cups milk
1½ teaspoons pure vanilla
6 Grade A large egg yolks
⅔ cup sugar
4 tablespoons all-purpose flour

Jackie's Chocolate Sauce

1. Prep work: Chop the chocolate into small pieces and set aside.

2. In a heavy saucepan, bring the milk and cream to the boil. Remove from heat. Add the chocolate, sugar, and butter and whisk until smooth.

3. Refrigerate any remaining sauce. Leftovers may be reheated.

8 ounces bittersweet or
*   semisweet chocolate*
¾ cup milk
¼ cup whipping cream
⅓ cup sugar
2½ tablespoons unsalted
*   butter at room*
*   temperature*

Makes 2 cups.

Gianduja Cannoli

When I met Jane Lavine at a New York Chocolate Festival, I was treated to a taste of a lacy hazelnut cannoli. Filled with a hazelnut mousse, it is a wonderful blend of flavors.

½ cup hazelnuts
½ cup unsalted butter at room temperature
⅓ cup dark brown sugar
¼ cup dark corn syrup
½ cup all-purpose flour
⅛ teaspoon salt
Gianduja Mousse Filling (recipe follows)

Serves 6.

You can substitute any kind of chocolate for the bittersweet Gianduja combination in this cannoli recipe. It would be very interesting to use Valrhôna Orange Lait Chocolate—hazelnut and orange are a wonderful combination.

1. Preheat the oven to 325°F. Lightly butter a baking sheet and set aside. Lightly oil 6 cannoli forms and set aside. (If you do not have cannoli forms, you can use a ¾-inch oiled wooden dowel.)

2. Prep work: Place the hazelnuts in a single layer on a baking sheet. Toast in oven for 15 minutes, until the nuts are evenly browned. Place nuts in a clean dish towel and rub off skins. Cool and chop fine in the bowl of a food processor fitted with a steel knife.

3. In a small saucepan, heat the butter, brown sugar, and corn syrup to simmering. Remove from heat and stir in the toasted nuts, flour, and salt. Stir until well combined. Bake 3 cookies at a time, using 1 tablespoon of batter for each cookie. Leave 4 inches between each cookie and 2 inches from the end of the baking sheet. Finished cookies will be approximately 3 inches in diameter.

4. Bake about 8 minutes or until cookies are dark brown and bubbling.

5. Remove pan from oven while cookies are still warm but pliable. Place cannoli form near one edge. Roll cookies one at a time onto form and transfer to wire rack. Repeat with remaining cookies. If cookies become too firm to roll, return pan to oven for 1 minute. When cookies are firm, gently remove forms. Repeat with rest of batter. Store uncovered on a wire rack until ready to fill. Fill a pastry bag, fitted with a medium star tip, with the Gianduja Mousse Filling. Pipe filling into each side of the cannoli. Refrigerate until serving time. Assemble just before serving. (Freezing is not recommended.)

Gianduja Mousse Filling

1. Prep work: Sprinkle the gelatin over the water in a small saucepan. Let stand until softened (about 5 minutes). Heat over very low heat until dissolved. Do not boil. Scald milk in a saucepan; stir in the gelatin. Keep warm over very low heat. Chop the chocolates into small pieces and set aside.

2. In the bowl of a food processor fitted with the steel blade, combine the chocolates, Frangelico, egg yolk, espresso powder, and salt. Process, scraping sides of bowl as necessary, until mixture is smooth. With machine running, add milk mixture in a steady stream. Process until incorporated. Transfer to a mixing bowl and cool to room temperature. Whip the cream until stiff peaks form. Mix a third into the chocolate mixture to lighten it, then fold in the rest. Chill until firm, about 4 hours.

¾ teaspoon unflavored gelatin
2 tablespoons water
½ cup milk
4 ounces Gianduja chocolate
2 ounces bittersweet chocolate
2 tablespoons Frangelico liqueur
1 Grade A large egg yolk
¼ teaspoon instant espresso coffee
⅛ teaspoon salt
½ cup whipping cream

12

Brownies

Brownies are high in sugar and butter content but with relatively little flour. They can be chewy or cakelike. Brownies can be a family treat or part of an elegant dessert table. The recipes in this chapter were selected to provide a broad range of tastes and textures. Interesting variations will result from changes in the chocolate used. Brownies are fun to bake. They can be made quickly and easily. They're great baking for an army of children because kids love 'em.

Tips for Baking Browies

- Use the correct pan size. They will not bake the same if batter is deeper or shallower.
- Spread the batter well into corners of the baking pan.
- Check timing carefully and begin testing for doneness 5–10 minutes before the suggested time. When done, the brownie will be springy when pressed lightly in the center and will pull away from the sides of the pan. A cake tester will come out clean.
- Use a sharp knife to cut cooled brownies; use a ruler, if necessary, to cut straight lines. If sticky, dip the knife in hot water.

Marbled Brownies

THE MARBLED APPEARANCE of this brownie is inviting. This one is yummy—satisfying without being overly sweet. It is a long-time family favorite. I wish I could remember where I found this recipe.

✴

4 ounces unsweetened chocolate
1 cup unsalted butter at room temperature
1 cup walnuts
4 Grade A large eggs, divided
2½ cups sugar, divided
1 cup all-purpose flour
½ teaspoon salt
2 teaspoons pure vanilla, divided
8 ounces cream cheese at room temperature

Makes approximately 30 brownies.

Have a brownie mélange when faced with unexpected company. Bake a different kind of brownie each time and save one or two from each batch. Wrap well, and keep in the freezer.

1. Preheat oven to 350°F. Butter and flour a 9-inch-by-13-inch baking pan and set aside.

2. Prep work: Chop the chocolate into small pieces. In a heavy saucepan over very low heat, melt the butter and chocolate, stirring constantly. When completely melted, remove from heat and set aside. Chop the nuts in the bowl of a food processor fitted with a steel knife, and set aside.

3. In a mixer bowl, beat 3 eggs until well blended. Slowly beat in 2 cups of the sugar and beat for 1 minute. Add the flour, salt, 1 teaspoon vanilla, and the nuts. Stop the mixer to scrape down the sides and bottom of the bowl to be sure all ingredients are well incorporated. Add the melted chocolate and mix well. Spread half the chocolate batter into the prepared pan. In another bowl, beat the cream cheese with the remaining ½ cup sugar until smooth. Add the remaining egg and vanilla and beat until thoroughly blended. Add half the white batter on top of the chocolate batter. Lightly swirl the batter in a crisscross pattern using the tip of a knife. Repeat with remaining batter.

4. Bake for 20 minutes, lower oven temperature to 325° and bake an additional 20 minutes, or until a toothpick inserted in the center comes out clean.

5. Allow brownies to cool in the pan on a rack. Cut into squares. (Brownies can be frozen in a single layer, provided they are well protected, with plastic wrap and then with aluminum foil.)

Pictured on color plate 6.

Chocolate Chip Brownie Bars

My NIECE LOVES TO BAKE **this for the family. Bari thinks they are the greatest—'cause it's a "chocolate chip cookie brownie." It takes just minutes to bake.**

1. Preheat oven to 375°F. Grease and flour a 9-inch square cake pan and set aside.

2. Prep work: Sift the flour, baking soda, and salt together and set aside. Chop the nuts in the bowl of a food processor fitted with a steel knife, and set aside.

3. Cream the sugar, brown sugar, butter, and vanilla in a mixer at high speed. Stop the mixer often to scrape down the sides and bottom of the bowl. Beat in the egg and mix well. Stir in the flour mixture until it just disappears. Stir in the nuts and chocolate chips. Because this is a thick dough, it must be pressed into the prepared pan with the fingers.

4. Bake about 20 minutes or until the top is nicely browned.

5. Allow brownie bars to cool in the pan on a rack. Cut into squares. (To freeze brownie bars, place in a single layer and protect well, first with plastic wrap and then with aluminum foil.)

1¼ cups all-purpose flour
½ teaspoon baking soda
½ teaspoon salt
½ cup walnuts
½ cup sugar
⅓ cup light brown sugar, firmly packed
½ cup unsalted butter at room temperature
1 teaspoon pure vanilla
1 Grade A large egg
6 ounces semisweet chocolate chips

Makes approximately 25 bars.

Susie Skoog's Chocolate-Caramel Brownies

THE CARAMEL ENHANCES the flavor of this brownie. They were created by Susie and became an immediate favorite. My mother loves them; you will too!

8 ounces block caramel
1 cup plus 2 tablespoons
  unsalted butter at room
  temperature, divided
¼ cup whipping cream
1 teaspoon pure vanilla
12 ounces semisweet
  chocolate
1⅓ cups sugar
6 Grade A large eggs
1 cup cake flour
Powdered sugar

*Makes approximately
20 brownies.*

1. Preheat oven to 350°F. Line a 9-inch-by-13-inch baking pan with parchment paper. Butter and flour the entire pan. *Preparation of the pan is important to make the brownies easy to remove.*

2. Prep work: In a heavy saucepan over low heat, stir the caramel, 2 tablespoons of the butter, the cream, and vanilla until the mixture is melted and smooth. Remove from heat and set aside. Chop the chocolate into small pieces and place in the top of a double boiler over hot, not boiling, water. Stir until chocolate is smooth; remove from heat and set aside.

3. Pour the chocolate into a mixing bowl. Beat 1 cup butter into the warm chocolate. (If the butter does not incorporate completely, set the pan over a low flame for a moment to finish the melting process.) Beat in the sugar. Add the eggs, one at a time, beating until the mixture lightens. Blend in the flour until it just disappears. Pour into the prepared pan. Slowly pour the caramel mixture over the chocolate batter, so it spreads evenly.

4. Bake 35 minutes or until a toothpick inserted 1 inch from the edge of the pan has a dry crumb.

5. Allow brownies to cool in the pan. Cut into long rectangles. Dust with powdered sugar. These are tricky brownies to get out of the pan because a thin layer of caramel settles on the bottom. Run a knife completely around the sides of the pan. Take a baking sheet and place it on top of the brownie pan, turn upside down, and lift off the brownie pan. Carefully peel the parchment paper. Place the brownies right side up on another baking sheet and dust again with powdered sugar. Cut into squares. (To freeze brownies, place in a single layer and protect well with plastic wrap, then with aluminum foil.)

Block Caramel is a product available in 5-pound blocks, made by the Nestlé Company. It is available from Madame Chocolate. It will set up with the addition of cream or butter. It can be melted in a microwave oven.

114

Bev Bennett's Brownies

THIS IS A GOOEY BROWNIE with a fudgelike consistency. It is a one-pot recipe from the food editor of the Chicago *Sun-Times*. Bev is certain this recipe once appeared in *Parade* magazine, but the brownies become identified with anyone who has the good taste to make them.

4 ounces unsweetened chocolate
3 Grade A large eggs
¾ cup all-purpose flour
1 cup unsalted butter at room temperature
2 cups sugar
1 teaspoon pure vanilla
1 cup nuts, chopped (optional)
Powdered sugar (optional)

Makes approximately 25 brownies.

1. Preheat oven to 350°F. Grease a 9-inch square cake pan and set aside.

2. Prep work: Chop chocolate fine and set aside. Lightly beat the eggs and set aside. Sift the flour and set aside.

3. Melt chocolate and butter in the top of a double boiler over hot, not boiling, water. Stir constantly and remove from heat when the chocolate is completely melted and smooth. Stir in the sugar, eggs, vanilla, flour, and nuts, and blend until smooth. Pour batter into the prepared pan.

4. Bake 35–40 minutes.

5. Allow brownies to cool in the pan on a rack. Cut into squares. Before serving, dust with powdered sugar. (To freeze brownies, place in a single layer and protect well, first with plastic wrap and then with aluminum foil.)

All of the brownies in this chapter can be frosted. Use Sharon's "Gram Helen" Chocolate Frosting, the Shiny Brownie Glaze, or any frosting or glaze listed in this book.

Nut Brownies

THE ELEGANT APPEARANCE of this brownie belies its simple one-pot preparation. It has a cakelike texture. I have been baking it since my children were very young, and it is one of my favorites.

꧁

1. Preheat oven to 350°F. Grease a 9-inch square cake pan and set aside.

2. Prep work: Chop chocolate fine and set aside. Lightly beat the eggs and set aside. Sift the flour, baking powder, and salt together and set aside. Chop nuts in the bowl of a food processor fitted with a steel knife, and set aside.

3. In a heavy saucepan, melt the chocolate and butter over low heat. Stir constantly, being careful not to burn the chocolate. When chocolate is completely melted and smooth, remove pan from heat. Stir in the sugar, vanilla, and eggs and blend until smooth. Stir in the flour mixture and blend well. Fold in the nuts. Pour batter into the prepared pan.

4. Bake 30–35 minutes.

5. Allow brownies to cool in the pan on a rack. Cut into squares. Before serving, dust with powdered sugar. (To freeze brownies, place in a single layer and protect well, first with plastic wrap and then with aluminum foil.)

5 ounces unsweetened chocolate
4 Grade A large eggs
1½ cups all-purpose flour
1 teaspoon baking powder
½ teaspoon salt
6 ounces pecans or walnuts
½ cup unsalted butter at room temperature
1½ cups sugar
1 teaspoon pure vanilla
Powdered sugar (optional)

Makes approximately 20 brownies.

San Quentin Fudge Bars

THIS BROWNIE BLENDS the tastes of brown sugar and nuts with the chocolate. It is easy to make. This recipe was provided by the Ghirardelli Chocolate Company.

※

2 Grade A large eggs
1 teaspoon pure vanilla
½ teaspoon salt
1 cup all-purpose flour
½ teaspoon baking powder
½ cup nuts
6 ounces Ghirardelli semisweet chocolate
¼ cup vegetable shortening
1 cup light brown sugar, firmly packed

Makes approximately 20 bars.

1. Preheat oven to 350°F. Butter a 9-inch square baking pan and set aside.

2. Prep work: Mix the eggs lightly in a bowl with the vanilla and salt and set aside. Sift the flour and baking powder together and set aside. Chop the nuts in the bowl of a food processor fitted with a steel knife, and set aside.

3. Chop the chocolate into small pieces and melt with the shortening, stirring occasionally until smooth. Remove the pan from the heat. Blend in the brown sugar. Stir the egg mixture into the melted chocolate. Add the flour mixture, all at once, beating until smooth. Pour batter into the prepared pan. Sprinkle the nuts on top.

4. Bake 18–20 minutes.

5. Allow brownies to cool in the pan on a rack. Cut into squares. (To freeze brownies, place in a single layer and protect well, first with plastic wrap and then with aluminum foil.)

Color Plates

Steve's Brownies

A DELIGHTFUL PHONE CALL brought this recipe from a pleased customer who claimed that it's the world's greatest brownie. It is a thin, fudgy brownie with a slight coconut taste.

꙼

1. Preheat oven to 325°F. Grease and flour a 9-inch-by-13-inch baking pan and set aside.

2. Prep work: Chop the chocolate into small pieces and put in the top of a double boiler over hot, not boiling, water. Add the butter, stirring until smooth, and remove from the heat. Chop the nuts in the bowl of a food processor fitted with a steel knife, and set aside.

3. In a mixer bowl, beat the eggs on low speed for 1 minute. Add the melted chocolate mixture, beating constantly. Beat in vanilla. Add sugar, flour, salt, nuts, and coconut. Beat only until combined. Pour into the prepared pan.

4. Bake for 25–30 minutes or until a toothpick inserted in the brownies is almost clean.

5. Allow brownies to cool in the pan on a rack. Cut into squares. (To freeze brownies, place in a single layer and protect well, first with plastic wrap and then with aluminum foil.)

Pictured on color plate 6.

3 ounces unsweetened chocolate
³/₄ cup unsalted butter at room temperature
¹/₂ cup nuts
4 Grade A large eggs
1 teaspoon pure vanilla
2 cups sugar
1 cup all-purpose flour
¹/₂ teaspoon salt
¹/₂ cup shredded coconut

Makes approximately 30 brownies.

Develop new and interesting tastes in brownies by changing the chocolate in the recipe. Bittersweet will give you the deepest chocolate taste; semisweet will give you a rich, sweet but chocolate taste; and milk chocolate will afford a more subtle taste.

Chocolate Chip Brownies

THIS DEEP CHOCOLATE cakey brownie is a chocoholic's delight. The chocolate chips enrich its taste.

3 ounces unsweetened
chocolate
8 tablespoons unsalted
butter at room
temperature
1 cup sugar
½ cup brown sugar,
firmly packed
½ cup light corn syrup
4 Grade A large eggs
1 cup bread flour
1 cup chocolate chips—
bittersweet, semisweet,
or milk chocolate
Powdered sugar
(optional)

**Makes approximately
30 brownies.**

1. Preheat oven to 375°F. Butter and flour a 9-inch-by-13-inch baking pan and set aside.

2. Prep work: Chop the chocolate into small pieces and melt in the top of a double boiler over hot, not boiling, water. Stir until smooth; remove from heat and set aside.

3. In a mixer bowl, cream the butter; add the sugar and brown sugar and beat for 2 minutes on high speed, until light and fluffy. Stop the mixer frequently to scrape down the sides and bottom of the bowl. Blend in corn syrup. Beat in the eggs, one at a time, until well incorporated. Stir in the melted chocolate, being sure the mixture is well blended. Gently fold in the flour and then the chips. Do not overmix! Pour into the prepared pan.

4. Bake 25–30 minutes.

5. Allow brownies to cool in the pan on a rack. Cut into squares. Dust with powdered sugar, if desired. (To freeze brownies, place in a single layer and protect them, first with plastic wrap and then with aluminum foil.)

Pictured on color plate 6.

Aileen's Brownies

CHOCOLATE CHIPS INTENSIFY the rich flavor of this delicate brownie. This is a very easy recipe that came from a very special friend, Aileen Shalowitz. By answering her "how-to" cooking questions she keeps me supplied with delicious recipes.

1. Preheat oven to 350°F. Butter and flour a 9-inch-by-13-inch baking pan and set aside.

2. Prep work: Chop the chocolate into small pieces and place with the butter in the top of a double boiler over hot, not boiling, water. Stir until very smooth and set aside. Chop the nuts and set aside.

3. In a mixer bowl, beat the eggs on medium speed until well blended. Slowly add the sugar, beating until it is well incorporated. Add the flour and vanilla. Stop mixer frequently to scrape down the sides and bottom of the bowl. Beat in the chocolate mixture. Fold in the chocolate chips and nuts with a spatula. Pour the batter into the prepared pan.

4. Bake about 25 minutes.

5. Allow brownies to cool in the pan on a rack. Cut into squares. Because these are delicate brownies, you may need to refrigerate them for an hour before removing them from the pan. (To freeze brownies, place in a single layer and protect well, first with plastic wrap and then with aluminum foil.)

4 ounces unsweetened chocolate
1 cup unsalted butter at room temperature
1 cup nuts (kind of nut is optional)
4 Grade A large eggs
2 cups sugar
1 cup all-purpose flour
1 teaspoon pure vanilla
1 cup semisweet chocolate chips

Makes approximately 45–50 brownies.

The full flavor of high quality chocolate will be lacking in some brands. Tasting will enable one to develop preferences.

Great Brownies

WHEN YOU LOVE TO BAKE, you want to be appreciated. A special young man in my life does just that. My nephew, David, is always anxious to taste. He loves this brownie recipe. While baking, the marshmallows disappear into the batter. The brownie can be dusted with powdered sugar or topped with a scoop of ice cream.

4 ounces unsweetened chocolate

1 cup pecans

1 cup unsalted butter at room temperature

2 cups sugar

4 Grade A large eggs

1 cup all-purpose flour

2 cups miniature marshmallows

1 tablespoon cognac or brandy

Powdered sugar (optional)

Makes approximately 30 brownies.

1. Preheat oven to 350°F. Butter and flour a 9-inch-by-13-inch baking pan and set aside.

2. Prep work: Chop the chocolate into small pieces and set aside. Chop pecans in the bowl of a food processor fitted with a steel knife, and set aside.

3. In the top of a double boiler over hot, not boiling, water, melt the chocolate and butter. Stir well until mixture is smooth. Remove pan from the heat and stir in the sugar. Beat in the eggs, one at a time, being sure each is incorporated before adding another. Stir in the flour, marshmallows, pecans, and cognac. Spread batter smoothly in the prepared pan.

4. Bake 30 minutes.

5. Allow brownies to cool in the pan on a rack. Cut into squares. When you are cutting them, use an up-and-down motion with your knife. (Do not drag your knife.) Chill in the refrigerator overnight. Serve cold or at room temperature. Dust with powdered sugar, if desired. (To freeze brownies, place in a single layer and protect well, first with plastic wrap and then with aluminum foil.)

Carol DeMasters' Pecan Brownies

CAROL is a professional food writer. This recipe is one of the first she learned to bake as a child. It will probably be the first recipe she will teach her daughter to bake. These brownies have a nice cocoa taste and are not very sweet. They have a crunchy texture and a very fudgy center.

1. Preheat oven to 350°F. Butter and flour a 9-inch-by-13-inch baking pan and set aside.

2. Prep work: Sift the cocoa and set aside. Sift the flour and set aside. Chop the nuts in the bowl of a food processor fitted with a steel knife, and set aside.

3. In a mixer bowl, cream the butter and gradually add the sugar. Beat on high speed for 5–10 minutes, until very light and fluffy. Stop the mixer often to scrape down the sides and bottom of the bowl. Add the cocoa and blend well. Add the eggs, one at a time, beating thoroughly after each addition. Blend in the flour, then the vanilla. Finally, fold in the nuts and pour batter into the prepared baking pan.

4. Bake 30 minutes or until a toothpick inserted in the brownies comes out just slightly moist.

5. Allow brownies to cool in the pan on a rack. Cut into squares. (To freeze brownies, place in a single layer and protect well, first with plastic wrap and then with aluminum foil.)

½ cup Dutch process unsweetened cocoa
1½ cups all-purpose flour
1 cup pecans
1 cup unsalted butter at room temperature
2 cups sugar
4 Grade A large eggs
1 teaspoon pure vanilla

Makes approximately 30 brownies.

The brownie recipes in this collection are deliciously different. Have a brownie party! Choose a recipe or two for each participant and come together for a tasting. After tasting, top the favorites with homemade ice cream.

Marbled Fudge Brownie Bars

THIS FUDGE BROWNIE IS well worth the time it takes to put the batter together. It has a delectable taste—like cheesecake marbled into a brownie. My house has always been the gathering place for my children and their friends, giving me a willing panel of tasters. This brownie has been on their hit parade for many years.

4 ounces semisweet chocolate

5 tablespoons unsalted butter at room temperature, divided

½ cup plus 1 tablespoon all-purpose flour, divided

½ teaspoon baking powder

¼ teaspoon salt

3 Grade A large eggs, divided

1½ teaspoons pure vanilla, divided

½ cup nuts

3 ounces cream cheese at room temperature

1 cup sugar, divided

¼ teaspoon almond extract

Makes approximately 20 brownies.

1. Preheat oven to 350°F. Butter and flour a 9-inch square cake pan and set aside.

2. Prep work: Chop the chocolate into small pieces and melt in the top of a double boiler over hot, not boiling, water with 3 tablespoons butter. Stir, making sure the mixture is smooth. Remove from the heat and cool slightly. Combine and sift ½ cup flour, the baking powder, and the salt and set aside. Mix 1 egg, 1 tablespoon flour, and ¼ teaspoon vanilla together in a small cup and set aside. Chop the nuts in the bowl of a food processor and set aside.

3. Make the white batter: In a mixer bowl, cream the remaining 2 tablespoons butter and the cream cheese until light and fluffy, gradually adding ¼ cup sugar. Mix in the egg, flour, and vanilla mixture. Stop the mixer frequently to scrape down the sides and bottom of the bowl. In another bowl, make the chocolate batter: Beat the remaining 2 eggs until thick and light in color. Gradually add remaining ¾ cup sugar, beating several minutes. Stir the sifted flour mixture into eggs. Blend in the remaining vanilla, the melted chocolate, nuts, and almond extract. Spread the chocolate batter in the prepared pan. Spread the white batter gently over the chocolate batter. Swirl with tip of a knife through the mixture to marble it.

4. Bake 25 minutes.

5. Allow brownies to cool in the pan. Cut into squares. (To freeze brownies, place in a single layer and protect well, first with plastic wrap and then with aluminum foil.)

Blond Brownies

THIS IS A LIGHT brownie, which is not as sweet as the others. This one-pot recipe is made with a small amount of chocolate chips. When I took my niece, Cindy, on a houseboat trip several years ago, I took along a selection of home-baked goodies. This is her favorite.

1. Preheat oven to 350°F. Set aside a 9-inch-by-13-inch baking pan. Do not butter it!

2. Prep work: Sift flour, baking powder, salt, and baking soda and set aside. Lightly beat eggs and set aside. Chop the nuts in the bowl of a food processor fitted with a steel knife, and set aside.

3. In a heavy saucepan, melt the butter. Stir in the brown sugar and allow mixture to cook over a medium flame for 1 minute. Remove the pan from the heat. Add eggs and vanilla to the pan and mix together well. Gradually beat in the flour mixture, mixing well after each addition. Spread batter in the ungreased pan. Sprinkle batter with the chocolate chips and nuts.

4. Bake 20–25 minutes.

5. Allow brownies to cool in the pan on a rack. Cut into squares. (To freeze brownies, place in a single layer and protect well, first with plastic wrap and then with aluminum foil.)

2 cups all-purpose flour
1 teaspoon baking powder
1 teaspoon salt
¼ teaspoon baking soda
2 Grade A large eggs
⅓ cup nuts
⅔ cup unsalted butter at room temperature
2 cups light brown sugar, firmly packed
2 teaspoons pure vanilla
6 ounces semisweet chocolate chips

Makes approximately 50 brownies.

Bittersweet chocolate chips can replace the semisweet chips suggested in this recipe to provide a deeper taste. Bittersweet chocolate chips are available from Madame Chocolate.

124

David's Brownies

A CLASSMATE OF MY SON, David, received a package of these delicious brownies. Aware of my constant search for outstanding recipes, David obtained the recipe. It is a delicious brownie. It ships well and will become a standard treat for sending to school or camp, or for keeping on hand.

½ *cup walnuts*
2 *ounces unsweetened*
  chocolate
¼ *pound unsalted butter*
  at room temperature
1 *cup sugar*
½ *cup all-purpose flour*
2 *Grade A large eggs*

Makes 25 small
brownies.

1. Preheat oven to 350°F. Butter an 8-inch square cake pan and set aside.

2. Prep work: Chop the walnuts in the bowl of a food processor fitted with a steel knife, and set aside.

3. Chop the chocolate into small pieces and melt with the butter in the top of a double boiler over hot, not boiling, water. Stir until smooth. Remove from the heat and stir in the sugar, then the flour, then the eggs, and then the nuts. Pour into prepared pan and smooth top.

4. Bake 20–25 minutes. Brownies will pull away from the sides of the pan.

5. Allow brownies to cool in the pan on a rack. Cut into squares. (To freeze brownies, place in a single layer and protect them, first with plastic wrap and then with aluminum foil.)

Pictured on color plate 6.

Shiny Brownie Glaze

THIS IS A SIMPLE RECIPE that can be used on
any brownie recipe in this book when a "dress-up" is
needed. The recipe comes from Jolene Worthington
and she also uses it on cookies.

---

1. Prep work: Chop the chocolate into small pieces
and set aside. Sift the powdered sugar and set aside.

2. Place the corn syrup, butter, and coffee in a heavy
saucepan. Bring the ingredients to a boil and add the
chocolate, stirring until smooth. Add powdered sugar
until the mixture is thick enough to spread. Use to glaze
brownies or cookies.

*6 ounces semisweet
chocolate*

*1½-2 cups powdered
sugar*

3 tablespoons corn syrup

*2 ounces unsalted butter
at room temperature*

*¼ cup brewed strong
coffee*

13

Cookies

The aroma of cookies baking arouses our desire to bake. Most baking careers start with the baking of chocolate chip cookies. As new and interesting cookie recipes are found, the desire to bake grows. Cookies are ideal as treats for special occasions, for sharing with family and friends, or for giving as gifts. Included among these recipes are many of my old favorites—enjoyed by my children as they grew up—and some new ones, too. With changes in the bits, pieces, and chunks of chocolate available today, all kinds of new recipes have been developed and passed along to me. I have tried all of them and have saved the best for you.

Tips for Baking Cookies

In any recipe, you can vary the size or shape of the chocolate piece used. With each change you make, you create a different-tasting cookie. Likewise, the flavor of the chocolate can be changed, substituting bittersweet for semisweet or milk. That, too, will change the taste of the cookie. I can only encourage you to experiment. You will be most pleased with the results.

- Be sure to use baking sheets that will allow air circulation in your oven.
- Grease sheets only when directed.
- Place the cookie dough on parchment paper sheets to make clean-up easier.
- Be sure to place dough on cool baking sheets.
- Have a sufficient number of baking sheets to make cookie baking easier.
- Wipe sheets with paper towels after each use if not using parchment paper.
- If you are baking more than one sheet at a time, switch oven positions at the halfway point.
- Use a timer and check cookies 2–3 minutes before the suggested baking time is up.
- Use a wide spatula to remove baked cookies from the baking sheet and always cool them on a wire rack.
- For drop cookies, use a small scoop to place dough on the baking sheets to assure evenly sized cookies. If you do not have a scoop, use a large pastry bag fitted with a large plain round tube and pipe the cookies onto the sheet.

- For rolled cookies, make sure the dough is rolled out on a cool surface.
- Flour your cookie cutters and move the cookies onto the pan with a spatula.
- For refrigerator cookies, make a round log and rotate log slightly with each slice so the bottom doesn't flatten.
- To make square refrigerator cookies, line a wax paper, foil, or plastic wrap box with plastic wrap and fill with dough. Level the top and chill until firm. Use a sharp knife to slice the cookies.

If Something Goes Wrong with Your Cookies

Cookies Do Not Spread

Dough overmixed
Too much flour
Oven temperature too high

Cookies Spread Too Much

Too little flour
Oven temperature too low
Baking sheet too heavily greased

Cookies Stick

Baking sheet not cleaned before use
Baking sheet not greased
Cookies allowed to cool for too long

Chocolate Frosted Drops

THIS IS A CAKELIKE cookie that can be enjoyed dusted with powdered sugar, frosted, or plain. As the cookies do not spread during baking, they can be baked in the size desired.

1. Preheat oven to 400°F. Set aside several ungreased baking sheets. (Line with parchment paper for ease in clean-up.)

2. Prep work: Sift the flour, baking soda, and salt and set aside. Chop the chocolate into small pieces and place in the top of a double boiler over hot, not boiling, water until melted. Stir until smooth and set aside. Chop the nuts in the bowl of a food processor fitted with a steel knife and set aside.

3. In a mixer bowl, cream butter and sugar for several minutes. Add egg, chocolate, water, and vanilla and beat until well blended. Stop the mixer often to scrape down the sides and bottom of the bowl. On low speed, add the flour mixture and the chopped nuts. Drop rounded teaspoons of dough onto the baking sheets.

4. Bake 8–10 minutes.

5. Cool cookies on a rack. Frost the cookies using a spatula to swirl the frosting. (These cookies can be frozen, provided they are well protected, first with plastic wrap and then with aluminum foil.)

1¾ cups all-purpose flour
½ teaspoon baking soda
½ teaspoon salt
2 ounces unsweetened chocolate
1 cup nuts
½ cup unsalted butter at room temperature
1 cup sugar
1 Grade A large egg
⅓ cup water
1 teaspoon pure vanilla
Chocolate Frosting (recipe follows)

Makes 48 cookies.

Chocolate Frosting

Chop the chocolate and place with the butter in a heavy saucepan over low heat. Stir until melted and smooth. Remove pan from heat and beat in the milk and powdered sugar until frosting is of spreading consistency.

2 ounces unsweetened chocolate
2 tablespoons unsalted butter at room temperature
3 tablespoons milk
2 cups powdered sugar

Pictured on color plate 7.

Chocolate Mint Chip Meringue Cookies

THIS IS MY DAUGHTER Jaime's favorite cookie. When she was very young she insisted on having them made in purple as well as green. For a long time, chocolate mint chips were unobtainable; now they can be purchased again. These cookies are also called "forgotten cookies" because they remain in the oven overnight.

3 Grade A large egg
  whites
1 teaspoon vinegar
1 cup sugar
Green food coloring
12 ounces chocolate mint
  chips

Makes 60 cookies.

A wonderful world of chocolate chips, bits, and pieces has opened up. The chocolate is available in various sizes—mini, maxi, and Buds, in addition to the familiar size; various sweetnesses— bittersweet, semisweet, milk chocolate, and mint; different shapes—slivers, chunks, wafers, and, of course, chips. They give an old recipe a new taste.

1. Preheat oven to 350°F. Line several baking sheets with parchment paper or a double thickness of wax paper. Set aside.

2. Prep work: Beat the egg whites until foamy; add the vinegar, and beat until almost stiff. Add the sugar a tablespoon at a time, beating on high speed for 5 minutes. To check to see if the meringue is ready, stop the mixer and rub a small amount of meringue between two fingers. The sugar should be dissolved and the mixture should feel smooth. Add just enough food coloring (paste, powder, or liquid) to obtain a pale green color. Fold in the chips. Drop meringue by teaspoonfuls onto the baking sheets. The cookies do not spread, so they can be dropped close together.

3. *Turn oven off.* Place the cookie sheets in the oven, leaving at least 6 hours or overnight. Cover tightly in an airtight container. Store in a cool, dry place.

Old-Fashioned Chocolate Cookies

THESE OLD-FASHIONED COOKIES are chewy and chocolaty. You'll adore them. They contain both chocolate and chocolate chips. My brother, Stanley, loves them when they are baked giant size.

꙼

1. Preheat oven to 350°F. Set aside several ungreased baking sheets. (Line with parchment paper for ease in clean-up.)

2. Prep work: Sift the flour, baking soda, and salt together and set aside. Chop the chocolate into small pieces and melt in the top of a double boiler over hot, not boiling, water. Stir until smooth and set aside. Chop the nuts in the bowl of a food processor fitted with a steel knife and set aside.

3. In the bowl of your mixer, cream the butter and both sugars together until light and fluffy. This will take several minutes on high speed. Beat in the egg and the melted chocolate. Beat in the flour mixture just until it disappears. Stir in the chips and nuts. Drop by tablespoonfuls 1½ inches apart on the cookie sheets. (For giant cookies use 2 tablespoons of dough.)

4. Bake 10 minutes. (For giant cookies bake 15 minutes.)

5. Cool cookies on a rack. (These cookies can be frozen, provided they are well protected, first with plastic wrap and then with aluminum foil.)

1 cup all-purpose flour
½ teaspoon baking soda
Pinch of salt
5 ounces semisweet chocolate
½ cup pecans
½ cup unsalted butter at room temperature
½ cup sugar
½ cup dark brown sugar, firmly packed
1 Grade A large egg
6 ounces semisweet chocolate chips

Makes 36 cookies.

Jane Salzfass Freiman's Chocolate Madeleines

A MADELEINE is a very special French sponge cookie, and a chocolate one is the best of all. Jane is a food writer and author of *The Art of Food Processor Cooking* (Contemporary Books). She has received national recognition for her syndicated food column. This cookie is perfect for the newly revived custom of having friends in for tea.

Vegetable oil
1 cup all-purpose flour
2 tablespoons
* unsweetened cocoa*
Pinch of salt
3 ounces semisweet
* chocolate*
¾ cup unsalted butter at
* room temperature*
4 Grade A large eggs
⅔ cup sugar
Powdered sugar for
* garnish*

Makes 24 madeleines.

There are several outstanding Dutch process unsweetened cocoas available today. The brands I recommend are: Ideal, Droste, Poulain, and DeZaan.

1. Preheat oven to 350°F. Adjust the oven rack to the middle position. Brush 2 number 80 madeleine pans lightly with vegetable oil and set aside.

2. Prep work: Combine the flour, cocoa, and salt. Sift together 3 times, and set aside. Chop the chocolate into small pieces and melt with the butter in the top of a double boiler over hot, not boiling, water. Stir well and set aside to cool.

3. Put eggs in a metal mixing bowl and set over, not in, simmering water. Gradually add sugar to eggs, whisking constantly until eggs feel warm to the touch. (Do not let eggs get too hot or they will scramble.) Remove from heat and pour into a mixer bowl. Beat on high speed until mixture is pale and thickened (4–8 minutes). Add the flour mixture and the chocolate mixture in one-third portions, beating on low speed until the flour disappears. Put a heaping tablespoonful of batter in each madeleine mold. Put pans side by side, but not touching, in the oven.

4. Bake 13–15 minutes or until a cake tester inserted in center of madeleine comes out clean.

5. Cool in the pan on a rack 15 minutes. Remove madeleines from the pans and allow them to continue cooling. Store in airtight tins. Sprinkle with powdered sugar before serving. (The madeleines can be frozen, provided they are well protected, first with plastic wrap and then with aluminum foil.)

Pictured on color plate 7.

Starlight Mint Surprise Cookies

A CHOCOLATE MINT WAFER is the surprise in this cookie. When my son, Steven, was a little boy, this was a popular cookie. But, mint wafers disappeared from the grocery shelves. The Ghirardelli Chocolate Company is now making them, and Steven is reliving his childhood memories.

1. Preheat oven to 375°F. Set aside several ungreased baking sheets. (Line with parchment paper for ease in clean-up.)

2. Prep work: Sift flour, baking soda, and salt together and set aside.

3. In a mixer bowl, cream the butter and both of the sugars until light and fluffy. This will take 5–10 minutes of beating at high speed. Beat in the eggs, water, and vanilla. Add the flour mixture slowly, stopping the mixer often to scrape down the sides and bottom of the bowl. Mix dough well. Shape into 1½-inch-diameter logs. Wrap in wax paper or plastic wrap and chill at least 4 hours. Cut log into ⅛-inch slices. Place half of the slices on the baking sheets. Top with a mint wafer, then with another dough slice. Pinch edges to seal. Top each with a walnut half, flat side down.

4. Bake 10–12 minutes or until nicely browned.

5. Cool cookies on a rack. (These cookies can be frozen, provided they are well protected, first with plastic wrap and then with aluminum foil.)

3 cups all-purpose flour
1 teaspoon baking soda
½ teaspoon salt
1 cup unsalted butter at room temperature
1 cup sugar
½ cup light brown sugar, firmly packed
2 Grade A large eggs
1 tablespoon water
1 teaspoon pure vanilla
8 ounces Ghirardelli mint wafers
40 walnut halves

Makes 40 cookies.

Use the Shiny Brown Glaze to "dress-up" cookies.

Choco-Nut Dainties

THIS·IS A NUT-COATED cookie recipe that was given to me by a student many years ago. I baked it many times for a little girl, the daughter of dearest friends. Now that Diane Schwartz is a young lady, she bakes this cookie and sends some to our house.

1 cup nuts
¾ cup plus 1 tablespoon unsalted butter at room temperature, divided
¾ cup sugar
1 Grade A large egg
1½ teaspoons pure vanilla
2 cups instant blending flour
1 teaspoon salt
1 tablespoon milk
12 ounces semisweet chocolate chips, divided

Makes 72 cookies.

1. Preheat oven to 350°F. Set aside several ungreased baking sheets. (Line with parchment paper for ease in clean-up.)

2. Prep work: In a food processor fitted with a steel blade, chop the nuts until they are even and fine. Use several on/off turns. Set aside.

3. In a mixer bowl, cream ¾ cup butter and the sugar together until light and fluffy. Add the egg and vanilla and blend well on high speed for 1 minute. Add the flour, salt, and milk and blend well. Stop the mixer frequently to scrape the sides and bottom of the bowl. Stir in half of the chips. Shape by hand into 2-inch-long logs. Place on the baking sheets about 2 inches apart.

4. Bake 14 minutes.

5. Cool cookies on a rack. Melt remaining chips and butter in the top of a double boiler over hot, not boiling, water until melted. If necessary, thin with a small amount of water. Stir until smooth. Dip one end of each cooled cookie in chocolate, then roll in the nuts. Place on wax paper until set. If a satiny chocolate gloss is desired, temper the chocolate in accordance with instructions given in Chapter 4. (These cookies can be frozen, provided they are well protected, first with plastic wrap and then with aluminum foil.)

Pictured on color plate 7.

The taste of this cookie can be varied by changing the sweetness of the chips used. The kind of nuts used also allows creativity.

Chocolate Lemon Cookies

THIS CHUNKY COOKIE HAS an irresistible, refreshing combination of flavors. It is a favorite in my house. Chocolate chunks have become very popular in cookie baking today.

※

1. Preheat oven to 400°F. Set aside several greased baking sheets. (Line with parchment paper for ease in clean-up.)

2. Prep work: Sift the flour, salt, and baking soda together and set aside. Roughly chop chocolate chunks and set aside.

3. In a mixer bowl at medium speed, cream the butter and the three sugars until light and fluffy. Beat in the egg, vanilla, lemon zest, and juice. Mix well. Stir the sifted flour mixture into the batter until it just disappears. Fold in the chocolate chunks. Drop by heaping teaspoonfuls 2 inches apart on the prepared sheets.

4. Bake 7–8 minutes or until the edges begin to brown.

5. Cool on a rack. (These cookies can be frozen, provided they are protected, first with plastic wrap and then with aluminum foil.)

1½ cups plus 1 tablespoon all-purpose flour
½ teaspoon salt
½ teaspoon baking soda
8 ounces bittersweet chocolate chunks
1 cup unsalted butter at room temperature
½ cup sugar
¼ cup light brown sugar, firmly packed
¼ cup dark brown sugar, firmly packed
1 Grade A large egg
1¼ teaspoons pure vanilla
Grated zest (rind) of 2 lemons
2 tablespoons fresh lemon juice

Makes 36 cookies.

The taste of these cookies can be changed by substituting Nestlé Burgundy (semisweet) chunks for the Nestlé Gibraltar (bittersweet) chunks in the recipe.

Peanut Chocolate Chip Monster Crisps

THE PEANUT-CHOCOLATE TASTE and crunchy texture make this a most delicious cookie. This is a monster cookie filled with extra-large chocolate chips.

꧁

3 cups all-purpose flour
$\frac{1}{2}$ teaspoon salt
$\frac{1}{2}$ teaspoon baking soda
$1\frac{1}{2}$ cups light brown sugar, firmly packed
$\frac{1}{2}$ cup unsalted butter at room temperature
$\frac{1}{2}$ cup vegetable shortening
2 Grade A large eggs
2 teaspoons pure vanilla
2 cups salted peanuts
12 ounces extra-large semisweet chocolate chips
Sugar

Makes 25–50 cookies.

1. Preheat the oven to 375°F. Set aside several greased baking sheets. (Line with parchment paper for ease in clean-up.)

2. Prep work: Sift the flour, salt, and baking soda together and set aside.

3. In a mixer bowl at medium speed, cream the light brown sugar, butter, shortening, eggs, and vanilla. Stir in flour until it is well blended. Stir in peanuts and extra-large chocolate chips. Drop rounded teaspoonfuls 2 inches apart, or rounded tablespoonfuls 3 to 4 inches apart, on the baking sheets. Sprinkle each cookie lightly with sugar.

4. Bake 8–10 minutes for teaspoon-sized cookies; increase baking time to 10–14 minutes for the larger cookies.

5. Cool cookies on rack. (These cookies can be frozen provided they are well protected, first with plastic wrap and then with aluminum foil.)

Vary the taste of the cookie by using extra-large milk chocolate chips.

Grandma's Chocolate Cookies

MY BROTHER STANLEY and I remember this cookie from our childhood. Grandma Rosie taught me how to bake this cookie before I could read. Now in her 90s, she loves to answer kitchen questions. If you're as lucky as I am, you will be able to remember the good baking smells of your home when you were a child.

1. Preheat the oven to 300°F. Set aside several ungreased baking sheets. (Line with parchment paper for ease in clean-up.)

2. Prep work: Sift the flour, baking powder, and salt together and set aside. Lightly beat eggs and set aside. Chop chocolate into small pieces and set aside.

3. Set a mixer bowl in a pan of hot, not boiling, water. Place chocolate and butter in the mixer bowl and let melt. Stir until smooth and then remove from heat. Return the bowl to the mixer and slowly add flour mixture to chocolate while mixing at low speed. Mix just until flour disappears. Mix in sugar and eggs and beat until well blended. Chill the dough until firm. Form dough into ¾-inch balls; roll in powdered sugar. Place 2 inches apart on the baking sheets.

4. Bake 18–20 minutes.

5. Cool on a rack. (The cookies can be frozen, provided they are well protected, first with plastic wrap and then with aluminum foil.)

2 cups all-purpose flour
2 teaspoons baking powder
½ teaspoon salt
4 Grade A large eggs
4 ounces unsweetened chocolate
½ cup unsalted butter at room temperature
2 cups sugar
Powdered sugar

Makes 50 cookies.

It is very important to use a fine quality unsweetened chocolate. Madame Chocolate sells several that will enhance your baking.

138

Chocolate Shot Cookies

THIS IS A BUTTERY COOKIE that melts in your mouth. My dear friend, Neil, tasted one and exclaimed, "Wow! I can eat all of them." Serve immediately after baking or you will finish them by yourself.

1½ cups all-purpose flour
½ teaspoon baking soda
1 cup unsalted butter at
*   room temperature*
1 cup powdered sugar
2 teaspoons pure vanilla
1 cup rolled oats
Pure chocolate shot

Makes 24 cookies.

1. Preheat the oven to 325°F. Set aside several un-greased baking sheets. (Line with parchment paper for ease in clean-up.)

2. Prep work: Sift the flour and baking soda together and set aside.

3. In a mixer bowl, cream the butter and powdered sugar until light and fluffy. Add vanilla and then the flour mixture. Blend well. Add the oats and mix thoroughly. Chill the dough for an hour and shape into 1½-inch-diameter logs. Roll the logs in the chocolate shot. Slice into ¼-inch slices and place 2 inches apart on the baking sheets.

4. Bake 20–25 minutes.

5. Cool cookies on a rack. (The cookies can be frozen, provided they are well protected, first with plastic wrap and then with aluminum foil.)

The chocolate shot suggested for these cookies is a pure chocolate, Swiss-made product. Madame Chocolate calls it vermicelli. It is also known as jimmies or sprinkles.

Skooger Doodles

THIS IS ANOTHER SUSIE Skoog kitchen
creation! She varied an old favorite for her children,
Cori, Oren, and Laura. The result is a delicious cookie
that is not too sweet.

1. Preheat oven to 400°F. Set aside several lightly
greased baking sheets. (Line with parchment paper for
ease in clean-up.)

2. Prep work: Mix sugar and cinnamon together in a
small bowl and set aside. Sift flour, cream of tartar,
baking soda, and salt together and set aside.

3. In a mixer bowl, cream the butter and shortening
together. Gradually add the sugar and beat until light
and fluffy. This will take several minutes. Stop the mixer
often to scrape down the sides and bottom of the bowl.
Add eggs, one at a time, beating well after each addition.
Add vanilla and blend well. Add flour mixture and mix
well into the dough. Stir in chocolate mini chips. Shape
dough into 1-inch balls; roll in cinnamon/sugar mixture and place 2 inches apart on the baking sheets.

4. Bake 10 minutes or until cookies are golden.

5. Cool cookies on a rack. (These cookies can be
frozen, provided they are well protected, first with plastic
wrap and then with aluminum foil.)

½ cup sugar
*2 tablespoons ground
  cinnamon*
2¾ cups all-purpose flour
*2 teaspoons cream of
  tartar*
1 teaspoon baking soda
½ teaspoon salt
*1 cup unsalted butter at
  room temperature*
*½ cup vegetable
  shortening*
1½ cups sugar
2 Grade A large eggs
1 teaspoon pure vanilla
*1 cup semisweet chocolate
  mini chips*

Makes 48 cookies.

*Our children come up
with great recipe
ideas. Listen carefully
to the next "Why
don't ya?" and try
doing it!*

Fudgy Morsels

THE FUDGY TASTE KEEPS this cookie among our favorites. They are delicious! I bake with a wonderful oven (Jenn-Air) that has a fan vented outside. As a result, my neighbors all know when I'm baking, Anne Weeks in particular. She has a nose for cookies, especially these.

1 cup all-purpose flour
½ teaspoon baking soda
⅛ teaspoon salt
5 ounces unsweetened chocolate
½ cup unsalted butter at room temperature
¼ cup dark corn syrup
⅓ cup light brown sugar, firmly packed
1 teaspoon pure vanilla
1 Grade A extra-large egg (or 1½ large eggs)

Makes 30 cookies.

Chocolate in its unsweetened form (chocolate liquor) is a most intense flavor. Addition of vanilla mellows and enhances the flavor of chocolate. This combination of chocolate and vanilla is used by bakers everywhere.

1. Preheat oven to 350°F. Set aside several greased baking sheets. (Line with parchment paper for ease in clean-up.)

2. Prep work: Sift the flour, baking soda, and salt together. Set aside. Chop the chocolate into small pieces and set aside

3. In a heavy saucepan over a very low flame, melt the butter, chocolate, corn syrup, brown sugar, and vanilla. Stir until the chocolate melts. Remove from the heat and let stand 10–15 minutes. Add egg and blend well. Add flour mixture and blend in. Place tablespoonfuls of batter 2 inches apart on the baking sheets.

4. Bake 10–12 minutes. Be careful that the bottoms do not burn.

5. Cool cookies on a rack. (The cookies can be frozen, provided they are well protected, first with plastic wrap and then with aluminum foil.)

Chocolate Coconut Chip Cookies

A LARGE OLD-FASHIONED cookie that is absolutely delicious. Everyone you bake them for will adore the taste.

1. Preheat oven to 375°F. Set aside several ungreased baking sheets. (Line with parchment paper for ease in clean-up.)

2. Prep work: Sift the flour, baking soda, and salt together and set aside.

3. In a mixer bowl, cream the butter and both sugars together until light and fluffy. Beat in the egg and vanilla. Stop mixer frequently and scrape down the sides and bottom of the bowl frequently while mixing. Beat in flour mixture until blended. Fold in oats, coconut, and extra-large milk chocolate chips. Drop by rounded teaspoonfuls 2 inches apart onto the prepared baking sheets.

4. Bake 12–15 minutes or until golden brown.

5. Cool the cookies on a rack. (These cookies can be frozen, provided they are well protected, first with plastic wrap and then with aluminum foil.)

1½ cups all-purpose flour
½ teaspoon baking soda
½ teaspoon salt
½ cup unsalted butter at room temperature
½ cup light brown sugar, firmly packed
⅓ cup sugar
1 Grade A large egg
1 teaspoon pure vanilla
1 cup rolled oats
1 cup flaked coconut
12 ounces extra-large milk chocolate chips

Makes 36 cookies.

You can reduce the sweetness of these cookies by substituting bittersweet or semisweet chocolate chips for the milk chocolate chips in the recipe.

Auntie Jane's Chocolate Chunk Cookies

AUNTIE JANE CREATED this recipe when chocolate chunks came on the market. She has been a fine baker for many, many years. I think baking keeps her young. I happily share this cookie with you.

½ cup bittersweet or semisweet chocolate chunks
¾ cup unsalted butter at room temperature
⅔ cup light brown sugar, firmly packed
½ cup sugar
2 tablespoons orange zest (colored part of the peel)
1 teaspoon pure vanilla
Pinch of salt
⅛ teaspoon baking soda
3 Grade A large eggs
1¼ cups all-purpose flour

Makes 48 cookies.

1. Preheat oven to 350°F. Set aside several ungreased baking sheets. (Line with parchment paper for ease in clean-up.)

2. Prep work: Chop the chocolate chunks into random pieces and set aside.

3. In a mixer bowl, cream the butter and both sugars until they are light and fluffy. Add orange zest, vanilla, and salt and beat well. Stir in baking soda, eggs, and flour. Be sure the mixture is well blended. Stir in the chocolate chunks. Drop by teaspoonfuls 4 inches apart onto the baking sheets.

4. Bake 10–12 minutes until a ¼-inch brown ring forms around the outer edge of the cookies.

5. Cool cookies on a rack. (The cookies can be frozen, provided they are well protected, first with plastic wrap and then with aluminum foil.)

Chocolate chunks are wonderful to use in cookies because they get soft but do not melt. You get a glob of chocolate in each bite.

Chocolate Raspberry Sandwich Cookies

THIS COOKIE WEDS the wonderful taste combination of chocolate and raspberry. The recipe comes from *The Food Enthusiast*™ (Box 205, Birmingham, MI 48012), an informative newsletter for "foodies" published by Yvonne Gill and Molly Hudson. This is Yvonne's recipe for a most tasty cookie.

1. Preheat oven to 350°F. Place rack in upper third of oven. Lightly grease several baking sheets and set aside. (Line with parchment paper for ease in clean-up.)

2. Prep work: Grate the chocolate very fine and set aside.

3. In a large bowl, mix the flour and sugar; cut in the butter. Make a well in the mixture and add the egg yolk. Top yolk with grated chocolate. Combine, using a palette knife; finish kneading with the heel of your hand so dough is an even chocolate color—not speckled. Form dough into a ball, flatten, and chill 20 minutes. (The unbaked dough may be refrigerated for 2 weeks or frozen.) Roll portions of the dough between 2 sheets of wax paper to ¼-inch thickness. Cut with a 2½-inch round, plain, or fluted cookie cutter. Cut ½-inch holes in the center of half of the rounds for the sandwich tops. Place rounds on prepared baking sheets.

4. Bake cookies, one sheet at a time, for 10–12 minutes.

5. Cool cookies on the sheets for 20 minutes. Spread preserves evenly over all of the cookie bases. Sift cocoa over the cookie tops. Place a top on each base, pressing down gently. Add an additional ¼ teaspoon of preserves in the center of each cookie. Melt the currant jelly in a small pan over low heat, stirring until it reaches 220°F. on a candy thermometer. Place a small amount of jelly in the center of each cookie. (These cookies keep very well and do not require freezing.)

Pictured on color plate 7.

4 ounces semisweet chocolate
2 cups all-purpose flour
3 tablespoons superfine sugar
¾ cup unsalted butter at room temperature
1 Grade A large egg yolk
1¼ cups raspberry preserves
4 tablespoons unsweetened cocoa
½ cup red currant jelly

Makes 30–35 cookies.

A variety of cookies can be made with this recipe by using different preserves. Strawberry, blueberry, black raspberry, apricot, and peach are among the flavors that are luscious with chocolate.

Rolled Cookies

Dip THIS COOKIE IN TEMPERED chocolate for an elegant appearance. This is a very versatile cookie. Variations are listed at the end of the recipe.

※

2 cups all-purpose flour
½ teaspoon salt
¾ cup plus 2 tablespoons unsalted butter at room temperature
1 cup sugar
1 Grade A large egg
1 teaspoon pure vanilla
Semisweet or bittersweet chocolate, melted and tempered (see directions in Chapter 4)

Makes about 30 cookies.

1. Preheat oven to 350°F. Set aside several ungreased baking sheets. (Line with parchment paper for ease in clean-up.)

2. Sift the flour and salt and set aside.

3. In a mixer bowl, cream butter and sugar until light and fluffy. Beat in the egg and vanilla. Gradually stir in the flour mixture. Be sure to mix well as the dough will be stiff. Wrap dough in plastic wrap and chill for 1 hour. Roll dough between 2 sheets of waxed paper to ¼-inch thickness. Cut with a 2-inch cookie cutter of your choice. Place on baking sheets.

4. Bake 10–12 minutes or until lightly browned around the edges.

5. Cool cookies on a rack. (Cookies can be frozen, before decorating, provided they are properly protected, first with plastic wrap and then with aluminum foil.)

Variations

Variation 1: Melt and temper chocolate (see index) and dip cookies either wholly or partly. Dipped cookies may be sprinkled with light or dark vermicelli or decor chips.

Variation 2: Dough can be rolled into logs and cut into ¼-inch slices. The cookie can be rolled into teaspoon-size balls and baked. They can be rolled in vermicelli before baking or baked with a chocolate Bud or wafer on top.

Variation 3: Make chocolate cookie dough, substitute ½ cup unsweetened cocoa for ¼ cup of flour specified in the recipe.

Variation 4: Make sandwiches filled with Chocolate Ganache (see index). Use baked cookies of the same size. Spread bottom cookie with an even layer of room temperature Ganache. Top with another cookie, pressing lightly. Dip as in Variation 1.

Have a chocolate cookie exchange with your friends. Invite twelve friends who are good cookie bakers. Ask each to bake and bring twelve dozen cookies to the party, using their favorite chocolate cookie recipe. Everyone goes home with one dozen of each cookie and voilà!—each will have a delicious and varied assortment of cookies.

Monster Cookies

SUSIE SKOOG CREATED THIS recipe especially for her children. They agreed to share their absolute favorite with you. Their mom always keeps a supply in the freezer and they eat them frozen. This recipe is monster size.

1 cup unsalted butter at room temperature
1½ pounds peanut butter
1 pound light brown sugar
2 cups granulated sugar
½ tablespoon light corn syrup
½ tablespoon pure vanilla
4 teaspoons baking soda
6 Grade A large eggs
1½ pounds semisweet chocolate chips
9 cups rolled oats

Makes 40–50 monster-sized cookies.

1. Preheat oven to 350°F. Set aside several ungreased baking sheets. (Line with parchment paper for ease in clean-up.)

2. In a mixer bowl, cream the butter and peanut butter together. Add the light brown sugar, sugar, corn syrup, vanilla, baking soda, eggs, chips, and rolled oats, one ingredient at a time, beating well after each addition. The mixture will become very stiff, and may have to be finished with your hands. Drop by giant tablespoonfuls onto the prepared baking sheet several inches apart.

3. Bake 10 minutes. The cookies will be a little soft when they first come out of the oven.

4. Cool on a rack. (These cookies can be frozen, provided they are well protected, first with plastic wrap and then with aluminum foil.)

Add sunflower seeds, raisins, nuts, granola, or coconut shreds to the monster cookies to make them more nutritious.

Chocolate Crinkle Cookies

THIS COOKIE IS AS MUCH FUN to bake as it is to eat. I came home one day to find my daughter, Jaime, baking it. Her friend Laura Cowan, gave her the recipe and told her of its great taste. It's a favorite in the Cowan house, the Sherman house, and it will be a favorite in your house.

1. Preheat oven to 350 degrees. Set aside several greased baking sheets. (Line with parchment paper for ease in clean-up.)

2. Prep work: Chop the chocolate into small pieces and melt in the top of a double boiler over hot, not boiling, water. Stir until melted and set aside. Sift the flour, salt, and baking powder together and set aside.

3. In a mixer bowl, combine the oil, melted chocolate, and sugar until well blended. Add the eggs, one at a time, mixing until each is well blended. Add the vanilla, then the flour mixture. Be sure the dough is well blended. Turn out onto a large piece of plastic wrap and chill overnight. Drop teaspoonfuls of the chilled dough into the powdered sugar. Place 2 inches apart on the prepared baking sheets.

4. Bake 10–12 minutes.

5. Cool cookies on a rack. (The cookies can be frozen, provided they are well protected, first with plastic wrap and then with aluminum foil.)

4 ounces unsweetened chocolate
2 cups all-purpose flour
½ teaspoon salt
2 teaspoons baking powder
½ cup corn oil
2 cups sugar
4 Grade A large eggs
2 teaspoons pure vanilla
1 cup powdered sugar

Makes about 60 cookies.

Here is a simple test for recipe evaluation: Is it made with chocolate? If so . . .

Peanut Butter Buds

THE CHOCOLATE BUDS IN THE center of these cookies add to the eye appeal of a cookie platter and make the cookies a delicious treat. The combination of chocolate and peanut butter is a long-time favorite of young and old.

✴

2⅔ cups all-purpose flour
2 teaspoons baking soda
1 teaspoon salt
1 cup unsalted butter at room temperature
⅔ cup peanut butter
1¾ cups sugar, divided
1 cup brown sugar, firmly packed
2 Grade A large eggs
2 teaspoons pure vanilla
60 milk chocolate Buds

Makes about 60 cookies.

1. Preheat the oven to 375°F. Set aside several ungreased baking sheets. (Line with parchment paper for ease in clean-up.)

2. Prep work: Sift flour, baking soda, and salt and set aside.

3. In a mixer bowl, cream the butter and peanut butter until smooth. Add 1 cup of sugar and the brown sugar and beat until creamy. Add the eggs and vanilla and blend well. Add flour mixture, mixing until blended. Shape the dough into 1-inch balls, roll in the remaining sugar and place on the prepared baking sheets.

4. Bake 8 minutes. Remove baking sheet from oven, place milk chocolate Bud in the middle of each cookie and bake for 2 additional minutes.

5. Cool cookies on a rack. (The cookies can be frozen if they are well protected, first with plastic wrap and then with aluminum foil.)

Chocolate Snowballs

A FESTIVE-LOOKING COOKIE, it is oft-requested at holiday time but can be a year-round treat. The Bud in the center is a chocolaty surprise.

※

1. Preheat oven to 375°F. Set aside several ungreased baking sheets. (Line with parchment paper for ease in clean-up.)

2. Prep work: Sift the flour and set aside. Chop the nuts to a fine powder in the bowl of a food processor fitted with a steel knife and set aside.

3. In a mixer bowl, cream butter and sugar until light and fluffy. Add vanilla, flour, and nuts blending well. Chill the dough for 2 hours. Using a tablespoon of dough for each cookie, shape it around each Bud, rolling in your hands until it forms a ball. Be sure Bud is completely covered. Place on prepared baking sheets.

4. Bake 12 minutes until cookies are set but not brown.

5. Allow cookies to cool slightly on a rack set over wax paper. Sift powdered sugar over tops of the cookies while still warm.(These cookies can be frozen, provided they are well protected, first with plastic wrap and then with aluminum foil. Allow the frozen cookies to return to room temperature, and roll in powdered sugar before serving.)

2 cups all-purpose flour
1 cup pecans
1 cup unsalted butter at
  room temperature
½ cup sugar
1 teaspoon pure vanilla
40 milk chocolate Buds
1 cup powdered sugar

Makes 40 cookies.

The Bud, made by the Wilbur Chocolate Company, is one of the oldest pieces of candy made in the United States. It is also available in semisweet chocolate which can be substituted for milk chocolate whenever a recipe calls for Buds. The Buds are available from Madame Chocolate.

14

Truffles and Candies

Gifts of homemade candy are doubly appreciated because the recipient of the gift knows that the effort of the giver is in each taste of the gift. Candy-making is as rewarding as the enjoyment of family and friends can be. If professional-looking chocolates are desired, chocolate must be tempered. Follow the instructions exactly and finished chocolates will be shiny, smooth, and not tacky to the touch. The extra effort is worth it.

Tips for Making Candy

- Make candy on a cool dry day.
- Do not double or halve a recipe; make several batches instead.
- Measure ingredients carefully to ensure the best results.
- Tempering chocolate for dipping requires proper preparation (directions can be found in Chapter 4). Once mastered, however, this technique is yours forever.
- Observe candy-making temperatures with an accurate chocolate or candymaking thermometer.
- Use high-quality tools and utensils.

Lutz Olkiewicz's Zurich Butter Truffles

LUTZ OLKIEWICZ OFFERED this recipe for a traditional Swiss truffle with a ragged look. Lutz is director of research and development for The Kitchens of Sara Lee. He was the executive pastry chef for Chicago's Drake Hotel for 25 years and has been a member of the United States Culinary Olympic Team.

1¼ pounds semisweet chocolate for centers
2 cups whipping cream
½ cup unsalted butter at room temperature
6 tablespoons sugar
6 tablespoons Grand Marnier
1½ pounds semisweet chocolate, tempered
¼ cup powdered sugar

Makes approximately 6 dozen truffles.

Madame Chocolate sells a great variety of ready-made boxes for packaging your homemade truffles, including beautiful gold and silver ballotins.

1. Chop 1¼ pounds of chocolate into ½-inch pieces and melt in the top of a double boiler over hot, not boiling, water. In a heavy saucepan, combine cream, butter, and sugar, bring to a boil over medium heat, stirring lightly to dissolve the sugar and blend all ingredients. Remove from heat and gently stir in the melted chocolate. Blend in liqueur. When chocolate mixture has cooled and thickened, spoon into a pastry bag fitted with a medium round tube and pipe bite-sized balls onto parchment or wax paper. Refrigerate until set. This is the center of the truffles.

2. While truffle centers are chilling, prepare the tempered chocolate. Place the 1½ pounds of chocolate in a clean, dry bowl. Pass bowl over a range burner (or place in the top of a double boiler filled with boiling water) and stir with your hand or a whisk until melting occurs on the bottom or sides of the bowl. Once melting starts, immediately remove the bowl from the heat. Stir a few more times and then return to the heat. Continue this process until mixture is thick and almost completely melted. Do not heat chocolate too fast or allow its temperature above 90°F. (A chocolate thermometer is required for proper tempering of chocolate.) If chocolate is overheated, it will be necessary to cool to an almost firm state and repeat the tempering process all over again. Let chocolate cool to 86°F., stirring constantly.

3. After centers have set and tempered chocolate is at the proper temperature, remove from the refrigerator and dust centers with powdered sugar. Dust your hands with powdered sugar, also. Roll centers into balls and, with a dipping fork, dip center into tempered chocolate.

Place dipped truffles onto a baking sheet covered with parchment paper. Return to refrigerator until set. Dip each truffle again into tempered chocolate and transfer immediately to a wire-mesh rack. Using a toothpick or a dipping fork, roll the truffles across mesh as chocolate sets, to produce traditional pointed markings. Store in an airtight container in refrigerator or freeze.

White Chocolate Truffles

THIS SIMPLE-TO-PREPARE TRUFFLE shows off the delicate flavor of white chocolate.

1. Preheat the oven to 300°F. Set aside a wax paper-lined baking sheet.

2. Prep work: Chop the white chocolate into small pieces and set aside. Toast the nuts on a baking sheet in a single layer for 5–8 minutes. Set them aside.

3. In the top of a double boiler over hot, not boiling, water, melt the white chocolate and the butter in the water. Stir until smooth. Pour into a bowl and add the yolk. Continue beating until the mixture is fluffy and cooled to room temperature. Chill until firm (about 4 hours). Remove from refrigerator and form into 24 1-inch balls. Sandwich between 2 nut halves. Chill until ready to serve.

8 ounces white chocolate (do not use compound coating)
48 perfect walnut or pecan halves
6 tablespoons unsalted butter at room temperature
1½ tablespoons water
1 Grade A large egg yolk

Makes 24 truffles.

Leslee Reis's Caramel Truffles

THIS CARAMEL TRUFFLE IS SERVED as an after-dinner treat to diners of Café Provençal. From its opening, this restaurant has regularly appeared on Chicagoland's best restaurant lists. Leslee Reis is the chef/owner of Café Provençal and the creator of this recipe.

1 pound bittersweet chocolate, tempered
1 package chocolate wafer cookies
½ cup sugar
½ cup water
2 tablespoons light corn syrup
2 tablespoons whipping cream
¾ cup unsalted butter at room temperature

Makes about 60 truffles.

1. Set aside several wax paper-lined baking sheets.

2. Prep work: Separate a ¼-pound chunk of the chocolate and chop the remaining ¾ pound into small pieces. Set all aside to temper when ready to dip centers. Crush the chocolate wafer cookies until they are very fine and set aside.

3. In a heavy saucepan over medium-high heat, place the sugar, water, and corn syrup. Cook, swirling the pan occasionally, to dissolve all the sugar. When the sugar is completely dissolved, discontinue stirring and let the syrup caramelize to the color of butterscotch. Remove pan from heat and add the cream and butter immediately. Stir until the mixture is completely smooth. Fill a large bowl halfway with ice water. Place the caramel pan in the ice water and stir constantly until cool and thick. Refrigerate until firm. Roll the firm caramel into balls slightly larger than a hazelnut. Refrigerate or freeze on a baking sheet until the centers are hardened.

4. Temper the chocolate. (See instructions in Chapter 4.) Using a dipping fork, dip each caramel center into the tempered chocolate and allow excess chocolate to drip off. Put on wax paper-lined baking sheet. Chill, if necessary, until chocolate hardens. Redip centers in the tempered chocolate and roll in the chocolate wafer crumbs to coat completely. Serve at room temperature.

Elaine González's Chocolate Truffles

"A TRUFFLE IS AN INTOXICATING morsel," says Elaine González, the author of *Chocolate Artistry* (Contemporary Books). This is a basic recipe from which variations to suit one's whims can be made.

❧

1. Set aside several wax paper-lined baking sheets.

2. Prep work: Separate a ¼-pound chunk of the semisweet chocolate and chop the remaining 2¾ pounds into small pieces. Set aside to temper when ready to dip. Chop the 12 ounces of chocolate into small pieces and set aside.

3. In a medium-sized heavy saucepan, over moderate heat, heat the cream until it simmers along the edges. Add the 12 ounces of chocolate and butter and stir until both are melted and the mixture is smooth. Set aside to cool briefly. When the mixture is lukewarm, add the pecans and cognac and stir to blend. Pour the mixture onto an ungreased baking sheet and chill it in the refrigerator or freezer until it is quite firm. Use a spoon, miniature ice cream scoop, or hands dusted with powdered sugar, to roll the cold, firm mixture into 1-inch balls, using a light, quick touch when handling them. Refrigerate or freeze the centers, uncovered, on a baking sheet until they are hard.

4. Temper the chocolate. (See instructions in Chapter 4.) Dip centers by hand or with a dipping fork in tempered semisweet chocolate. Place on wax paper to set.

3 pounds semisweet chocolate, for tempering
12 ounces semisweet chocolate, for centers
1 cup whipping cream
4 tablespoons unsalted butter at room temperature
1 cup chopped pecans
1 tablespoon cognac

▬▬▬▬▬▬▬▬▬▬

Truffles can be topped with: a pecan; walnut half; an almond; hazelnut; glacéed fruit; crystallized flowers; chocolate coffee bean; vermicelli; or decor chips, if done before the chocolate dries. The truffles can be rolled in: cocoa powder, powdered sugar, coconut, finely chopped nuts, or cookie crumbs.

▬▬▬▬▬▬▬▬▬▬

Michael Bortz's Grand Marnier Truffles

THE DELICIOUS, sensual truffles of Michael Bortz are on the cover of this book. Michael is the owner/chocolatier of Mill Acres, a gourmet shop, in Wyomissing, Pennsylvania. His handmade chocolate work is both exquisite and ambrosial. His crème fraîche truffles are available from Madame Chocolate's catalog.

2 pounds semisweet chocolate, tempered
1 pound milk chocolate, for centers
¾ cup whipping cream
1 ounce unsalted butter at room temperature
1 ounce sugar
2 ounces Grand Marnier
1 teaspoon natural orange flavor (extract)
1 Grade A large egg yolk
Cocoa powder

Makes 48 truffles.

1. Set aside several wax paper-lined baking sheets.
2. Prep work: Separate a ¼-pound chunk of the semisweet chocolate and chop the remaining 1¾ pounds into small pieces. Set aside to temper when ready to dip.
3. Chop the milk chocolate into small pieces and place in a mixing bowl. In a heavy saucepan over medium heat, bring the cream, butter, and sugar to a boil. Pour the hot mixture over the chocolate and mix until the chocolate melts and the mixture is smooth. Add the Grand Marnier, the orange flavor, and the egg yolk and mix until blended and smooth. Pour mixture into a mixer bowl, cover, and chill until firm (about 2 hours). Remove the bowl from the refrigerator and beat at moderate speed for 3–5 minutes, until the mixture becomes the consistency of pie dough. Roll in ¾-inch balls and place on the prepared baking sheets. Chill the centers for 30 minutes.
4. Temper the chocolate. (See instructions in Chapter 4.) Using a dipping fork, dip the centers into the tempered semisweet chocolate. Roll in cocoa powder. (The truffles will keep one week at 65°F. and do not require refrigeration.)

Variations

Variation 1: The Grand Marnier may be replaced by another liqueur: amaretto, Kahlua, Framboise, Frangelico, etc.

Variation 2: The orange flavoring may be replaced by another flavoring or extract: vanilla, lemon, peppermint, brewed strong coffee. (Avoid flavorings that are not compatible with liqueur.)

Variation 3: Enhance the truffle mixture with ½ cup of finely chopped nuts, glacéed fruit, crystallized ginger, etc.

Variation 4: Roll truffles in finely chopped nuts, ground cookie crumbs, powdered sugar, etc.

Truffles are great as gifts for special people. Enhance your gift with an elegant container. Use wicker, china, or a crystal basket, or pack in a candy dish, pretty box, decorative tin, transparent jar, or a container molded from chocolate.

Million-Dollar Fudge

THIS IS A VERY OLD RECIPE adapted for *The Fanny Farmer Cookbook* (Knopf), by my dear friend, Marion Cunningham. It is a recipe that is easy enough for children to make.

∗|∗

12 ounces semisweet chocolate
1 cup marshmallow cream
2 cups sugar
1 tablespoon unsalted butter at room temperature
¾ cup evaporated milk
⅛ teaspoon salt
1 teaspoon pure vanilla
1 cup chopped nuts

Makes 36 pieces.

1. Oil a 9-inch square pan and set aside.

2. Prep work: Chop the chocolate into small pieces and place it, along with the marshmallow cream in a large bowl and set aside.

3. In a heavy saucepan over low heat, mix the sugar, butter, and milk, stirring to combine well. Gradually bring the milk mixture to a boil, stirring until the sugar dissolves. Dip a pastry brush into cold water and wash down the sides of the pan. Continue to boil, stirring constantly without touching the sides of the pan, for 5 minutes. Pour mixture over the chocolate mixture and add the salt and vanilla. Stir until the chocolate melts and the mixture is smooth, then stir in the nuts. Spread into the prepared pan.

4. Let fudge stand until firm. Cut into 1½-inch squares and store in an airtight container.

Opera House Chocolate Fudge

Fudge is an all-american treat, and this is a delicious easy-to-make recipe. I am grateful to the Ghirardelli Chocolate Company for this recipe. Ghirardelli is one of the oldest American chocolate manufacturers and they told me that this recipe came about soon after the company's founding.

1. Butter an 8-inch square pan and set aside.

2. Prep work: Chop the chocolate into small pieces and set aside.

3. In a heavy saucepan, over low heat, combine the half and half, chocolate, light corn syrup, sugar, and salt. Stir well until smooth. Heat to a boil, over medium heat, then lower the heat and cook uncovered, without stirring, to the soft ball stage (325°F. on a candy thermometer) or about 25 minutes. Remove from heat. Add butter to pan but do not stir. Cool mixture to room temperature. Stir in vanilla. Beat until fudge thickens. Stir in nuts. Spread in the prepared pan.

4. Chill until set. Cut into squares to serve

4 ounces Ghirardelli unsweetened chocolate
⅔ cup half and half cream
1 tablespoon light corn syrup
2 cups sugar
¼ teaspoon salt
1 tablespoon unsalted butter at room temperature
1 teaspoon pure vanilla
¾ cup chopped nuts

Makes 25 pieces.

Chocolate Ripple Divinity

THIS IS AN EASY-TO-MAKE confection. It will make the kitchen novice appear to have many years of kitchen candy-making experience. It is also an ideal holiday gift from your kitchen.

⚜

6 ounces semisweet chocolate
2 cups sugar
½ cup water
½ cup light corn syrup
⅛ teaspoon salt
2 Grade A large egg whites
1 teaspoon pure vanilla

Makes 50.

Vary the sweetness and brand of chocolate in your fudge and candy recipes and you'll create a brand new taste. Using bittersweet chocolate, your fudge will be less sweet and more chocolaty tasting. Don't overlook white chocolate, Gianduja, or Orange Lait chocolates for making fudge.

1. Set aside a wax paper-lined baking sheet. Butter the wax paper.

2. Prep work: Shave the chocolate with a knife or a vegetable peeler and set aside.

3. In a medium-sized heavy saucepan over low heat, mix the sugar, water, corn syrup, and salt, stirring until the sugar dissolves. With a pastry brush dipped in cold water, wipe any crystals from the sides of the pan. Cook to 262°F. (almost to soft crack stage, use a candy thermometer) without stirring. Beat the whites until stiff. When the syrup reaches the proper temperature, pour it over the whites, beating constantly. Add the vanilla; beat until mixture loses its gloss and holds peaks. Fold in the chocolate. Drop by teaspoonfuls onto the prepared baking sheets.

Frozen Chocolate Caramel Bananas

THIS RECIPE IS FOR children of all ages. Made with fine caramel and wonderful chocolate, it will bring back childhood memories.

~✲~

1. Set aside a wax paper-lined baking sheet.

2. Prep work: Separate a ¼-pound chunk of the semisweet chocolate and chop the remaining ¾ pound and set aside to temper when ready to dip bananas. Peel the bananas and cut them in half crosswise. Insert a stick into the cut end of each banana and freeze them.

3. In a heavy saucepan over low heat, melt the caramel, stirring until smooth. When smooth, stir in the peanut butter and allow mixture to cool. Dip each banana into the caramel mixture. Use your hand to press caramel onto banana. When completely covered, roll the banana in the peanuts; place on the wax paper and freeze. Temper the chocolate (see instructions in Chapter 4) and, when the caramel banana is frozen, dip in the tempered chocolate, allowing excess to drip off. Place on prepared baking sheet. Freeze until ready to serve.

1 pound semisweet chocolate, tempered
6 firm, ripe bananas
14 ounces block caramel
½ cup peanut butter
12 4½-inch-long candy sticks
1 cup chopped peanuts

Makes 12 bananas.

Cornflake Delight

THIS RECIPE IS QUICK AND easy to make. It is an old recipe that evolved when cornflakes were the only cereal available. You can substitute the cereal of your choice to vary the recipe.

∿

2 pounds semisweet chocolate
10 cups cornflakes
½ cup salted peanuts
2 cups maple syrup
2 cups sugar
2 cups peanut butter

Makes 40.

1. Butter a 9-inch-by-13-inch baking pan and set aside. Set aside a wax paper-lined baking sheet.

2. Prep work: Separate a ¼-pound chunk of the semisweet chocolate and chop the remaining 1¾ pounds into small pieces and set aside to temper when ready to dip centers. Place the cornflakes and the peanuts in a mixing bowl and set aside.

3. In a heavy saucepan, bring the maple syrup and the sugar to a boil; remove from heat and stir in the peanut butter. Stir until smooth. Pour the mixture over the cornflakes and stir until well mixed. Pour into the buttered baking pan. Cool until set. Cut into pieces.

4. Temper the chocolate. (See instructions in Chapter 4.) Using a dipping fork, dip the cornflake squares into the tempered chocolate. Allow excess chocolate to drip off. Place on wax paper until set.

Chocolate Pecan Caramel Treats

THIS CANDY HAS MANY NAMES. **It is a best-seller for most chocolate confectioners. It is easy to make and loved by all.**

1. Set aside a lightly buttered baking sheet.

2. Prep work: Separate a ¼-pound chunk of the semisweet chocolate and chop the remaining 1¼ pounds into small pieces and set aside to temper when ready to dip candies.

3. In the top of a double boiler over hot, not boiling, water, melt the caramel in the cream. Stir until smooth and let cool 10 minutes. Arrange pecan halves in groups of three on the prepared baking sheet. Spoon a tablespoon of caramel mixture over nuts, leaving the tips uncovered. Let stand for 30 minutes.

4. Temper the chocolate. (See instructions in Chapter 4.) Dip the caramel pecan piece in the tempered chocolate; place on baking sheet to set. Caramel treats keep well at room temperature. Protect with plastic wrap, if necessary.

1½ pounds semisweet chocolate
8 ounces block caramel
2 tablespoons whipping cream
1¼ pounds pecan halves

Makes 24 pieces.

15

Sauces

❧

Sauces are used to enhance the taste and eye appeal of cakes, mousses, brownies, and ice cream (homemade, of course). This is a collection of the most palate-pleasing sauces you've ever tasted. Each recipe stands on its own merits and its own chocolate taste. Do not overlook the taste of a chocolate sauce with poached fruit; it makes a simple dessert simply elegant. Try the sauces in a pool around a scoop of chocolate or white chocolate mousse, around a thin slice of cake or torte, or simply eat them with a spoon!

Tips for Making Sauces

- Using a heavy saucepan will diffuse the heat evenly and prevent the sauce from scorching.
- Sauces will keep for several days in the refrigerator, provided they are well covered. They are best rewarmed in a double boiler, but a microwave oven will work well, too. Do not heat them too much or they will separate.

Easy Fudge Sauce

THIS SAUCE IS AN all-around favorite! It's dark, thick, smooth, and not too sweet. It takes just minutes from start to finish.

‑‑‑

16 ounces semisweet
   chocolate
½ cup whipping cream
⅓ cup water

Makes 2¼ cups.

1. Prep work: Chop the chocolate into small pieces and set aside.
2. In a heavy saucepan, bring the cream and water to a boil. Add the chocolate and stir over a very low flame until completely melted. Use a whisk to stir and dissolve any remaining small pieces.
3. Serve warm or at room temperature. Store in the refrigerator. Leftovers can be reheated.

Fudge Sauce

PUT THIS SAUCE on top of a Chocolate Chocolate-Chip brownie and listen to the moans. What a way to go! This sauce is dark, thick, and has the deep taste of cocoa.

6 tablespoons unsalted
   butter at room
   temperature
1 cup unsweetened Dutch
   process cocoa
1 cup whipping cream
⅔ cup sugar
1 cup light brown sugar,
   firmly packed
Pinch of salt
1 teaspoon pure vanilla

Makes 2½ cups.

1. Prep work: Cut the butter into pieces and set aside. Sift the cocoa and set aside.
2. In a heavy saucepan over medium heat, stir the cream and butter until the butter melts and cream bubbles around the edges. Stir in both sugars until dissolved. Lower heat. With a whisk, stir in the salt and cocoa. Let boil a few seconds and remove from heat. Add vanilla and stir until smooth.
3. Sauce can be served hot or cold. Store in the refrigerator. Reheat sauce in the top of a double boiler over hot, not boiling, water.

Sauce Hot Fudge Cordon Rose

THIS RECIPE was created by Rose Levy Beranbaum for the Poulain Chocolate Company to show off its bittersweet baking chocolate. Rose runs the Cordon Rose Cooking School in New York City and is expert at working with chocolate.

※

1. Prep work: Chop the chocolate into small pieces and set aside.

2. In a heavy saucepan over low heat, melt the chocolate in the water, stirring constantly. Add the butter, sugar, and light corn syrup and bring to a boil, stirring constantly. Let the mixture simmer 10–15 minutes or until it thickens. Do not stir during this time. The mixture will reduce to about 1¼ cups. Remove pan from the heat and stir in the vanilla and salt. Stir until smooth.

3. Sauce should be served warm. Store in tightly covered, heatproof jar, in the refrigerator. Before using, place jar in simmering water until sauce is warm. Leftovers can be warmed the same day.

3¾ ounces Poulain bittersweet chocolate (12 logs)
⅔ cup water
¼ cup unsalted butter at room temperature
⅓ cup sugar
¼ cup light corn syrup
1 teaspoon pure vanilla
Pinch of salt

Makes 1¼ cups.

Have a "Get Sauced" party. Prepare a variety of sauces. Vary the sweetness and brands of chocolate used. Keep the sauces warm on an electric hot tray and serve with homemade ice cream.

Nancy Harris's Chocolate Sauce

NANCY HARRIS HAS FOUND many uses for this sauce in catering on Chicago's North Shore. It is a thin sauce and should be used in small amounts with simple desserts. It is excellent with poached fruit or over chocolate crêpes. Try it in other ways also.

9 ounces bittersweet chocolate
1 cup water
⅓ cup sugar
1 tablespoon cognac, brandy, amaretto, crème de menthe, any other liqueur of your choice, or 1 tablespoon pure vanilla

Makes 2 cups.

1. Prep work: Chop the chocolate into small pieces and set aside.

2. In a heavy saucepan over low heat, stir the water and sugar until the sugar dissolves. Remove from heat; add the chocolate and stir until melted. Return pan to low heat and stir constantly with a whisk for about 2 minutes. Remove from heat and cool slightly. Stir in the cognac, liqueur, or vanilla.

3. Sauce may be served warm or at room temperature. Store in refrigerator. Leftovers can be reheated.

Pictured on color plate 8.

Hot Fudge Sauce

THIS WONDERFUL FUDGE sauce has a very rich cocoa taste. Use it on ice cream, cake, or just eat it with a spoon.

½ cup unsalted butter at room temperature
1 cup unsweetened Dutch process cocoa
¾ cup sugar
½ cup light brown sugar, firmly packed
⅛ teaspoon salt
1 cup whipping cream
1 teaspoon pure vanilla

Makes 2½ cups.

1. Prep work: Cut the butter into pieces and set aside.

2. In a heavy saucepan, add the cocoa, both sugars, and the salt. Add the cream and butter; stir constantly with a whisk over low heat. Bring to a boil; allow to boil 1 minute. Remove pan from the heat and cool 5 minutes. Stir in the vanilla extract. Blend until smooth.

3. Sauce can be served warm or at room temperature. Store in the refrigerator. Leftovers can be reheated.

Susie Skoog's White Chocolate Apricot Sauce

SUSIE SKOOG DEVELOPED THIS sauce in keeping with the modern trend for lightness. This is a most interesting and delicious use of white chocolate.

1. Prep work: Chop the white chocolate into small pieces and set aside.

2. In a heavy saucepan, melt the butter in the water. Bring to a boil, stirring constantly. Lower heat; add the white chocolate and continue to stir until the mixture is completely smooth. Add the corn syrup and preserves. Bring to a boil and boil gently about 5 minutes. Strain and stir until smooth.

3. Sauce should be served warm. Store in the refrigerator. Leftovers can be reheated.

3 ounces white chocolate (do not use compound coating)
6 tablespoons unsalted butter at room temperature
½ cup water
2 tablespoons light corn syrup
½ cup apricot preserves

Makes 1¼ cups.

Peach or pineapple preserves make delicious white chocolate sauces. For a quick and easy dessert, top a slice of chocolate pound cake with chocolate ice cream and your favorite white chocolate dessert sauce.

Thick Orange Milk Chocolate Sauce

IF YOU LIKE THE combination of orange and chocolate, you will adore this sauce. Not only does it taste good; it smells divine. It is delicious with poached pears or with most of the chocolate cakes in the book. You can vary the sauce by using semisweet or bittersweet chocolate.

4 ounces Orange Lait
(orange milk chocolate)
½ cup milk
⅓ cup sugar
¼ cup unsalted butter at
room temperature
1 teaspoon pure vanilla
1 teaspoon baking soda
Pinch of salt

Makes 1¾ cups.

1. Prep work: Chop the chocolate into small pieces and set aside. Heat the milk to simmer and set aside. Have a double boiler ready to use.

2. In the bowl of a food processor, fitted with a steel blade, place the sugar and chocolate. Mix with several on/off turns, then process an additional minute. Add the butter; process 1 minute. With the machine running, pour the hot milk through the feed tube and process 30 seconds. Add the vanilla, baking soda, and salt and process 30 seconds. Pour sauce into the top of a double boiler over hot, not boiling, water and heat until the sugar is completely dissolved, stirring occasionally. Remove from heat and stir until smooth.

3. Sauce should be served hot. Store in the refrigerator. Leftovers can be reheated.

Poached fruit is delicious with fudge sauce on it. Poach apples, pears, peaches, nectarines, etc. in simple syrup. Serve with chocolate sauce. It's a fresh, new approach.

Luscious Chocolate Almond Sauce

THE NESTLÉ KITCHENS provided this smooth, creamy sauce. It combines the flavor of chocolate with almond. ⤳

1. In a heavy saucepan over low heat, combine 6 ounces mini-morsels, cream, butter, and salt. Stir constantly until morsels melt and mixture is smooth. Bring just to a boil and remove from heat. Add liqueur and blend well.

2. Serve warm over ice cream. Sprinkle remaining mini-morsels on top. Store remaining sauce in the refrigerator. Leftover sauce may be reheated.

12 ounces Nestlé semisweet chocolate mini-morsels, divided
¼ cup whipping cream
2 tablespoons unsalted butter at room temperature
⅛ teaspoon salt
3 tablespoons almond-flavored liqueur

Makes 1 cup.

Sharon's "Gram Helen" Chocolate Frosting

THIS IS A MOST delicious, easy frosting. It can be used on anything you wish to frost: cakes, brownies, cookies, your arm, etc. ⤳

1. Prep work: Chop the chocolate into small pieces and set aside.

2. In the top of a double boiler over hot, not boiling, water, melt the chocolate, butter, and sugar together. Stir until chocolate has melted and the sugar is dissolved. Remove from heat and whisk in the egg. Whisk in the cream, vanilla, and salt. Stir until smooth.

3. Refrigerate the frosting until spreadable.

3 ounces semisweet chocolate
¼ cup unsalted butter at room temperature
¼ cup sugar
1 Grade A large egg
⅓ cup whipping cream
1 teaspoon pure vanilla
Pinch of salt

Makes 1 cup.

16

Other Indulgences

This is a group of recipes that includes everything from crêpes, coffeecakes, terrines and pâtés, to puddings. Each one will bring joy to your life and those who will be invited to dine at your table. They are unique recipes and, of course, they are all chocolate. Old recipes will seem brand new again if good chocolate is used, and varied from time to time.

TIPS

- Read each recipe carefully.
- Follow the directions because the recipes work as they are written here.
- If baking is required check your oven with an accurate oven thermometer.
- Use the right-sized pans and check for doneness about 5–10 minutes before the end of the suggested baking time.
- Allow sufficient time for refrigeration or freezing, if required. If they need to be warmed before serving allow enough time for that, too.

Barbara Tuleja's Terrine of Bittersweet Chocolate with Fruits and Nuts

BARBARA CONCEIVED THIS as a delicious alternative to the holiday fruitcake. It can be made in different shapes and sizes for holiday gifts. As an example of Barbara's creativity, she serves it on mirror glass with artfully arranged fresh fruit. This is a recipe with an outstanding presentation and will serve a large group.

1 teaspoon almond or safflower oil
8 ounces semisweet chocolate
8 ounces bittersweet chocolate
½ cup dried apricots
¼ cup dried pineapple
¼ cup dried papaya
8 ounces unsalted butter at room temperature
¼ cup Kahlua
1 Grade A large egg
2 Grade A large egg yolks
½ cup whole hazelnuts
½ cup whole glacéed red cherries
20 blanched whole almonds
20 glacéed cherries (optional)
10 cups fresh tart fruit: raspberries, orange and tangerine sections, fresh pineapple spears, kiwi fruit and persimmon slices, red currants, or tart red cherries (optional, for garnish)

Serves 16–20.

1. Line a covered terrine, approximately 10 inches long by 3 inches wide by 2½ inches high, with a double thickness of plastic wrap, molding the wrap tightly to the sides and crevices of the terrine with your fingers and leaving a 2-inch overhang on all sides. Paint the plastic wrap with a thin film of almond oil using a pastry brush and set it aside.

2. Prep work: Bring all ingredients to room temperature. Chop the chocolate into small pieces and set aside. Dice the apricots, pineapple, and papaya into ¼-inch cubes and set aside.

3. In the bowl of a food processor fitted with a steel knife, process the semisweet and bittersweet chocolate for approximately 30 seconds to the powdery, irregular small bead stage, scraping down the sides of the bowl as necessary. In a small pan, melt the butter, without allowing it to take on any color. Add Kahlua, and heat to 180°F., checking the temperature on an instant reading thermometer. With the processor running, immediately pour the hot butter mixture through the feed tube, processing until completely amalgamated. Add egg and egg yolks and process for 5 more seconds. Working quickly, transfer chocolate mixture to prepared terrine and gently mix in the diced and whole dried fruits and hazelnuts, keeping fruit and nuts away from the sides of the terrine. Smooth top of terrine and knock the bottom, soundly, once or twice against a hard surface to eliminate the air pockets and settle the contents. Cover the terrine.

4. Refrigerate for 12 hours until completely firm. At serving time, gently pull plastic wrap from the walls of the terrine to free all sides. Transfer terrine to a serving platter (or a large mirror), holding it by the overhangs. Remove the plastic wrap and decorate the top with whole almonds and glacéed cherries. Slice into $\frac{1}{4}$-inch slices with a thin, sharp knife, leaving approximately one-third of the terrine whole. Arrange cut slices in an overlapping pattern and surround terrine with fresh fruit.

5. The dessert will keep, refrigerated and tightly wrapped, for up to 4 days.

A wonderful chocolate and fruit buffet may include: Susie Skoog's Chocolate Cherry Cake, Chocolate Lemon Cookies, Barbara Tuleja's Terrine of Bittersweet Chocolate with Fruits and Nuts, Jackie Etcheber's Banana Tart, Chocolate Strawberry Fool, Steve's Brownies, Chocolate Raspberry Sandwich Cookies, and Perla Meyers' Chocolate Marquise with Pear Sauce.

Michael Bortz's Gianduja Bombe

MICHAEL BORTZ is the owner of Mill Acres in Wyomissing, Pennsylvania, a gourmet food shop with a wonderful pastry department. It owes its fine reputation to Michael's talent as a chocolatier. His truffles grace the cover of this book (see index) and his hazelnut chocolate bombe will pay honor to your taste buds.

Chocolate Sponge Roll (recipe follows)
20 ounces Gianduja chocolate, divided
1 ounce hazelnuts
1 cup plus 5 ounces whipping cream, divided
4 ounces Crème Fraîche (see index)
4 ounces unsalted butter at room temperature

Serves 10–12.

1. Line a 6-cup (8-inch-diameter) bowl with plastic wrap. Cut the following pieces out of the baked Chocolate Sponge Roll: a 7-inch circle, a 3½-inch circle, and 7 wedges, 3½ inches across the top, 1½ inches across the bottom, and 3¾ inches high. (Make this pattern from cardboard, use to cut the cake pieces, and save pattern for future use.) Use cake pieces to line the bowl, saving the 7-inch circle for the top. Set aside.

2. Prep work: Chop the Gianduja chocolate into small pieces and set aside. In the oven, place the hazelnuts on a baking sheet in a single layer and toast for 15 minutes, until brown. Place nuts in a clean dish towel and rub off the skins. Place the nuts in the bowl of your food processor, fitted with the steel blade, and process until finely chopped. Set aside.

3. Place 12 ounces of the Gianduja in a mixing bowl. In a medium saucepan, bring 5 ounces of cream to a boil. Remove from heat and pour over Gianduja and whisk until the chocolate is melted and smooth. Whip the remaining cream and the Crème Fraîche together until almost stiff. Carefully fold the hazelnuts, chocolate, and whipped cream together until the mixture is well blended. Pour into the prepared cake-lined bowl and top with the 7-inch cake.

4. Freeze the bombe for a minimum of 4 hours or overnight. Be sure it is well covered with plastic wrap. Unmold onto a serving plate and remove the plastic wrap that lined the bowl. Protect the plate with 4 pieces of wax paper placed slightly under the bombe. Place the remaining 8 ounces of Gianduja in a small bowl. Heat the butter and pour over the Gianduja, whisking until melted and smooth. Pour this glaze over the whole surface of the mold using a small offset spatula to help, if necessary. Remove the wax paper and decorate the bombe with chocolate clay roses (see Elaine González's *Chocolate Artistry* for instructions), or whipped cream. (The bombe can be frozen, unglazed, provided it is well protected, first with plastic wrap and then with aluminum foil.)

The Bombe may be made with bittersweet, semisweet, or milk chocolate, if desired. White chocolate or Orange Lait could also be used.

Elaine González's Chocolate Sponge Roll

THIS RECIPE IS PROVIDED by Elaine González, author of *Chocolate Artistry* (Contemporary Books). Her book is the first and last word in decorating with chocolate and is a must for the kitchen of any choco-chef. Elaine is a chocolate artist and an excellent teacher.

¼ cup sugar
⅛ cup all-purpose flour
⅛ cup cornstarch
¼ cup unsweetened Dutch process cocoa
5 Grade A large eggs
⅛ teaspoon salt
1 teaspoon pure vanilla

1. Preheat oven to 350°F. Grease and flour an 11-inch-by-17-inch baking pan. Line the pan with wax paper or parchment paper; grease and flour the paper. Set aside.

2. Prep work: Sift the sugar, flour, cornstarch, and cocoa together several times and set it aside. Separate the eggs and set the bowls aside.

3. In a small bowl, beat the yolks until they are thick and lemon-colored. Place the whites in a large grease-free bowl. Add the salt and beat until the mixture is quite stiff but not dry. Transfer it to a large shallow bowl to facilitate the next step. Use a rubber spatula to fold the thickly beaten yolks lightly into the whites. Fold the dry ingredients into the mixture in about 4 additions. Fold in the vanilla last. Pour mixture into the prepared pan and smooth the surface evenly with an offset metal spatula.

4. Bake 12–15 minutes or until the cake tests done. (It will spring back when touched in the center.) Do not overbake.

5. Allow cake to cool in the pan about 5 minutes before removing. Loosen the sides of the pan with a sharp knife. Invert the cake onto a wax paper-covered cake rack and continue to cool it. Remove the baking paper and replace it with a sheet of aluminum foil. Invert the cake again (top side facing up) and cool. (The sponge freezes well, provided it is well protected, first with plastic wrap and then with aluminum foil.)

Chocolate Chip Coffee Ring

THE EYE-OPENING TASTE OF this coffee ring is great for starting the day. It is an easy-to-make recipe.

❧

1. Preheat oven to 350°F. Grease a 9-inch tube pan and set aside.

2. Prep work: In the bowl of a food processor fitted with a steel knife, chop the walnuts. In a mixing bowl, combine ¼ cup flour, brown sugar, and cocoa. Cut in 2 tablespoons butter until the mixture resembles coarse crumbs. Add the walnuts and set aside.

3. In a mixer bowl, on medium speed, beat the sugar with the remaining ½ cup butter until light and fluffy. Add the remaining 2 cups of flour and blend well. Add the sour cream, eggs, baking powder, baking soda, and vanilla and beat at low speed until blended. Continue beating for 3 to 4 minutes at medium speed, stopping the mixer to scrape sides and bottom of bowl. Stir in the chocolate chips. Pour the batter into the pan and smooth the top. Crumble the walnut mixture evenly over the batter.

4. Bake 40-45 minutes or until cake pulls away from the sides of the pan.

5. Allow cake to cool in the pan on a rack. Loosen cake from pan using a small metal spatula. Invert cake onto serving plate. (Coffee cake may be frozen, provided it is well protected, first with plastic wrap and then with aluminum foil.)

¼ cup walnuts
2¼ cups flour, divided
¼ cup light brown sugar, firmly packed
1 teaspoon unsweetened Dutch process cocoa
½ cup plus 2 tablespoons unsalted butter at room temperature, divided
1 cup sugar
1 cup sour cream
2 Grade A large eggs
1 teaspoon baking powder
1 teaspoon baking soda
1 teaspoon pure vanilla
8 ounces semisweet chocolate chips

Serves 10–12.

Dee Coutelle's Chewy, Gooey Chocolate Crêpes

DEE CREATED THIS RECIPE for the first Hyattfest Chocolate Weekend. It was a huge success with people who had been eating chocolate for more than a day. Try these crêpes at home for brunch, dessert, or a late evening snack. Let your guests choose from the fillings you serve.

2 Grade A large eggs
2 tablespoons plus 1 teaspoon unsalted butter at room temperature, divided
⅓ cup all-purpose flour
2 teaspoons sugar
2 tablespoons unsweetened Dutch process cocoa
¼ cup Crème Fraîche (recipe follows)
¼ cup water
Cherry Orange Filling (recipe follows)
Chocolate Orange Filling (recipe follows)
Pear Filling (recipe follows)

Makes 8 crêpes.

1. A well-seasoned 8-inch crêpe pan is required.

2. Prep work: Beat eggs lightly and set aside. Melt butter and set aside.

3. Sift flour, sugar, and cocoa into a bowl. Beat in Crème Fraîche, water, and eggs until smooth. Stir in 2 tablespoons of the melted butter. Let batter rest 1–2 hours in the refrigerator or refrigerate overnight and bring back to room temperature. Stir batter; if it has thickened, add a few drops of water.

4. Prepare pan: Heat to medium, painting with the remaining butter. (When a drop of water skips over the surface, the pan is ready.) Add a 3-tablespoon portion (¼ cup of batter) to center of pan. Rotate to spread it around evenly. Cook about 35–40 seconds. Flip crêpe over for just a few seconds. Stack on a plate. Separate with wax paper if saving for later use. Fill crêpes with one of the following fillings, as instructed below. The sauces can be kept for several days in tightly sealed containers. (You can refrigerate or freeze crêpes, provided they are well protected, first with plastic wrap and then with aluminum foil.)

Crème Fraîche

Mix the cream and buttermilk and heat in a saucepan to 75°F. Place in a partially covered glass jar and leave at room temperature for 12 hours. Cover and refrigerate. May be kept for 2 weeks.

1 cup non-ultra-pasteurized whipping cream
½ cup buttermilk

Cherry Orange Filling

1. Preheat oven to 325°F. Butter a baking dish and set aside.

2. Before you begin: Drain and chop cherries and set aside (save ½ cup cherry juice). Grate the chocolate and set aside.

3. In a heavy saucepan, combine powdered sugar and cornstarch. Stir in liqueur, lemon juice, and cherry juice. Add cherries and stir over medium heat until thickened (about 8-10 minutes).

4. Spoon cherry filling over half the crêpe (making a semicircle), leaving 1 inch of the outer circumference dry (as the filling will spread when the crêpe is folded). Fold crêpe in half and then in half again, making a triangular shape. Place crêpes in the prepared dish.

5. Bake for 10 minutes. Put Crème Fraîche and grated chocolate on top. Serve immediately. Crêpes can be prepared and filled earlier for finish when ready.

2 16-ounce cans pitted, dark sweet cherries
1 ounce semisweet chocolate
½ cup juice from canned cherries
1 cup powdered sugar
1½ tablespoons cornstarch
½ cup orange liqueur
1 teaspoon fresh lemon juice
1 cup Crème Fraîche (recipe above)

Chocolate Orange Filling

4 ounces semisweet
chocolate

6 tablespoons Crème
Fraîche

½ cup sweetened
condensed milk

3 tablespoons orange
liqueur or rum, divided

2 tablespoons orange
marmalade

1 cup whipping cream

2 teaspoons grated orange
zest

1. Chop the chocolate into small pieces and place in a small saucepan. Melt the chocolate and add the Crème Fraîche and milk, stirring constantly. Add 1 tablespoon liqueur and the marmalade. Blend well. Fill crêpes and bake as in previous recipe.

2. For topping: Place whipping cream, orange zest, and 2 tablespoons liqueur in a bowl. Place bowl in a larger bowl of ice water. Whip with a whisk until the cream mounds softly and leaves streaks when beaters are pulled through. Do not overbeat or cream will become grainy and lose its shine. Refrigerate for 1–2 hours or use immediately.

Pear Filling

1. Peel, then split the pears lengthwise to remove tough core. Rub with ½ lemon to keep white. Quarter pears lengthwise and slice into ⅛-inch-thick slices. Place in bowl of water acidulated with the juice of one lemon. When all pears are prepared, drain them. Melt butter in a sauté pan; add pears and sauté until pears are soft, adding liqueur during cooking. Cover with lid askew. If pears are watery, remove lid and cook to evaporate water. It may take 20 minutes, depending on the firmness of the fresh pears. Add sugars at the end of cooking, stirring until dissolved. Fill and bake as in preceding recipe.

2. Sprinkle cooked crêpes with powdered or granulated sugar before serving.

4–6 very ripe pears
1½ lemons, divided
3 tablespoons unsalted butter at room temperature
1 tablespoon pear liqueur or orange liqueur
3 tablespoons sugar
3 tablespoons powdered sugar
Powdered sugar for topping

Chocolate Swirl Coffee Cake

THIS RECIPE WAS developed by the Nestlé Kitchens. They graciously allowed me to share it. It is a wonderful yeast coffee cake swirled with chocolate and cinnamon. It's enjoyable any time of day or night.

4¼ cups all-purpose flour, divided

1 cup plus 2 tablespoons sugar, divided

1½ teaspoons cinnamon, divided

¾ cup butter at room temperature, divided

1 cup Nestlé Toll House semisweet chocolate morsels, divided

¼ cup chopped nuts

½ cup water

⅓ cup milk

1 teaspoon salt

2 packages active dry yeast

2 Grade A large eggs

⅓ cup evaporated milk

Serves 12–14.

1. Preheat oven to 350°F. Grease a 10-inch tube pan and set aside.

2. Prep work: In a small bowl, combine ¼ cup of the flour, ¼ cup of the sugar, and 1 teaspoon of the cinnamon. Cut in ¼ cup butter until mixture resembles coarse crumbs. Stir in ¼ cup chocolate morsels and the nuts. Set this streusel topping aside until needed.

3. In a heavy saucepan over medium heat, combine ¾ cup sugar, water, milk, ½ cup butter, and salt. Heat, stirring constantly, until all ingredients are smooth. Allow to cool to 130°F. (This is absolutely necessary to avoid killing the yeast.) While liquid is cooling, combine 1½ cups flour and the yeast in a separate bowl. Add the cooled liquid to the flour mixture. Add eggs and mix well. By hand, stir in 2½ cups of flour to make a moderately soft dough. Place dough in a greased bowl and let rise until doubled in volume (about 2 hours). Punch down; turn out on a lightly floured surface; cover with plastic wrap; and let rise 10 minutes. While waiting, the swirl can be made: In the top of a double boiler over hot, not boiling, water, combine ¾ cup chocolate morsels, evaporated milk, 2 tablespoons sugar, and ½ teaspoon cinnamon. Heat until chocolate melts and mixture is smooth. Allow mixture to cool to lukewarm while rolling dough into an 18-inch-by-10-inch rectangle. Spread with chocolate swirl mixture. Roll up jelly-roll-style from long end. Join ends and pinch together. Place in the prepared tube pan. Sprinkle streusel on dough. Let rise until doubled in volume (about 1¼ hours).

4. Bake 45–50 minutes.

5. Allow to cool in the pan for 15 minutes, then remove from pan and allow to cool completely. (Coffee cake can be frozen if well protected, first with plastic wrap and then with aluminum foil.)

Dee Coutelle's Chocolate Yeast Scones

D EE COUTELLE IS ONE of Chicago's outstanding cooking teachers. She also tests foods and recipes and is regularly coming up with new ideas. This recipe for scones is one of her best. This chocolate-drizzled scone is delicious.

2 cups all-purpose flour
½ teaspoon salt
2 tablespoons plus 2 teaspoons sugar, divided
8 tablespoons warm water (100° F.), divided
2 teaspoons active dry yeast
¼ cup lard (fresh is highly preferred)
7 tablespoons unsalted butter at room temperature, divided
¾ cup decor chips

Makes 15 scones.

1. Preheat oven to 400°F. Position rack in the center of the oven. Set aside several buttered and floured baking sheets.

2. Prep work: Mix the flour and salt in a large mixing bowl. Dissolve 2 teaspoons of the sugar in 6 tablespoons of the warm water. Sprinkle yeast over the water and set aside 5 minutes or until the mixture foams, indicating the yeast is active. Set the mixtures aside.

3. Mix the remaining 2 tablespoons water with the remaining 2 tablespoons sugar. Stir the yeast mixture and the sugar/water mixture into the flour to make a dough. Knead until the dough is smooth and elastic (about 5 minutes). Form dough into a ball; place in a straight-sided bowl and cover with plastic wrap. Let rise until double in volume (about 2 hours). Cut up lard using a dough scraper. Using heel of hand and dough scraper, gather and spread lard into a mass and set aside. Follow the same procedure to soften the butter and set aside. Roll dough into a 14-inch-by-9-inch rectangle with the 9-inch sides at the top and bottom. Spread upper third of rectangle with softened lard and sprinkle with ¼ cup decor chips. Fold upper third of dough over

center third and fold bottom third up as if folding a letter. Turn dough rectangle so that flap faces right. Roll dough into a 14-inch-by-9-inch rectangle; again spread top third of dough with 3 tablespoons of butter. Sprinkle with ¼ cup decor chips; fold as before. Turn flap to right. Roll a third time to 14-inch-by-9-inch rectangle. Spread top third of dough with 3 tablespoons butter and sprinkle with remaining chips. Fold as before and turn flap to right. Roll to 12-inch-by-5½-inch rectangle that is ½ inch thick. Cut 10 circles of dough using a 2¼-inch round cookie cutter and place on prepared baking sheets. Dough scraps can be used by placing side by side, not on top of each other. Dampen edges of dough with water and press to seal. Spread 1 tablespoon butter over upper third of 4-inch-by-6-inch rectangle that is made utilizing scraps. Fold as above; turn flap to right; roll to ½-inch thickness; cut out additional circles from that dough; place on baking sheet. Let rise until nearly doubled in volume, about 1 hour.

4. Bake 20 minutes.

5. Serve hot with butter or preserves or drizzle with melted semisweet chocolate. (Do not freeze dough or scones.)

Barbara Kafka's Chocolate Sorbet

THIS IS A SIMPLE, delicious recipe. The sorbet can be made with any kind of ice cream maker. Barbara created this light, but rich tasting dessert to satisfy our chocolate craving. Barbara delights in all matters of taste.

6 ounces unsweetened chocolate
6 cups water, divided
3 cups sugar

Makes 8 cups.

1. Prep work: Chop the chocolate into small pieces and set aside.

2. In a large, heavy saucepan over medium heat, place chocolate and 1 cup water. Stir occasionally to make a smooth mixture. As the chocolate mixture thickens, gradually add another cup of water, ½ cup at a time. When mixture is completely smooth and melted, add remaining water and the sugar. Stir until sugar is dissolved. Cook over medium heat for 15–20 minutes but do not boil. Remove from heat, allow to cool, then pour mixture into ice cream machine and freeze according to directions. If you do not have an ice cream maker, freeze in the following manner: Pour mixture into a large baking pan. Let cool at room temperature about 10 minutes. Place in the freezer and freeze until very hard. It will take about 5 hours. Stir mixture frequently as it freezes. About 1 hour before serving, break up mixture or put cubes of it into a food processor fitted with a steel knife and process until smooth. Return to freezer, stirring occasionally before serving.

Every time you vary the brand and sweetness of the chocolate you use, you vary the taste of the sorbet. It would please Barbara if you would experiment, for her greatest joy is teaching people how to taste.

Albicocca Cioccolato (Chocolate Apricot Gelato)

189

THE MOST OUTSTANDING ice cream in Chicagoland is made by Al Gelato, a west suburban "gelateria." Their ice creams are made from secret family recipes. Mike Winter, one of the owners, provides a recipe that tastes very much like "the real thing."

1. Prepare your ice cream maker according to manufacturer's directions.

2. Prep work: Chop the chocolate into very fine pieces and set aside. Cut the apricots into ¼-inch dice and set aside.

3. In a heavy saucepan place the eggs and sugar. In another saucepan combine the cream and milk and heat to a simmer. Slowly whisk the simmering cream into the egg yolks. Stir 5–6 minutes over low heat, until mixture thickens slightly. Place the chocolate in a mixing bowl. Slowly stir in the hot, thickened cream mixture until the chocolate is melted and smooth. Set aside until cool. Refrigerate until completely chilled, about 1 hour or longer. Just before churning ice cream, stir diced apricots into the chilled chocolate cream.

4. Pour into an ice cream dasher and follow manufacturer's directions for freezing.

5. Ice cream must be kept in the freezer. It's hard to understand why it evaporates from my freezer.

8 ounces semisweet chocolate
4 ounces dried apricots
6 Grade A large egg yolks
1¼ cups sugar
1 cup whipping cream
2 cups milk

Makes slightly more than 1 quart.

Unlimited possibilities arise in ice cream making. One could substitute any kind of dried fruit for the apricots. Add fresh fruit, nuts, chocolate chips, chunks of chocolate, cookie crumbs, etc. Suit your fancy!

190

Abby Mandel's Boule de Neige

Aʙʙʏ MANDEL IS NATIONALLY acclaimed for her food processor recipes. Her books and her magazine and newspaper columns have established her as a preeminent cooking personality. Abby created this chocolate snowball. With its eye appeal equaled by its taste appeal, it will enhance your dessert table.

8 ounces semisweet
  chocolate
8 ounces unsalted butter
  at room temperature
1 cup whipping cream
1 cup plus 2 tablespoons
  sugar, divided
2 teaspoons instant coffee
  powder
½ cup boiling water
4 Grade A large eggs
1 tablespoon plus 2
  teaspoons cognac or
  dark rum, divided
6 candied violets

Serves 8–12.

1. Fifteen minutes before baking, place the rack in the center of the oven and preheat to 350°F. Line a 5-cup ovenproof bowl or soufflé dish with a double thickness of foil, extending the edges beyond the sides of the dish (first shape the foil over the outside of the dish; then it will fit neatly inside). A deep round dish will give the finished snowball a round shape.

2. Prep work: Chop the chocolate into small pieces and set aside. Cut the butter into 12 pieces and set aside. Chill the cream.

3. In the bowl of a food processor fitted with the steel knife, pulse the chocolate with 1 cup sugar and coffee 4 times, then process continuously until the chocolate is as fine as the sugar. With the machine running, pour the boiling water through the feed tube and process until the chocolate is melted, stopping once to remove cover and scrape down bowl. Add butter and process an additional minute. Add eggs and 1 tablespoon cognac or rum and process 15 seconds. Pour into the prepared dish.

4. Bake about 1 hour or until the surface is puffy and cracked and covered with a thick crust.

5. Set the dish on a rack to cool. The mixture will recede as it cools. When completely cool, remove the snowball from the dish by the extensions of foil and wrap airtight in the foil. Refrigerate for several hours or overnight until the mixture is firm. Invert onto a serving plate and peel off the foil. The chocolate will appear sticky and irregular. Whip the cream until thick, then add the 2 tablespoons sugar and remaining cognac or rum. Place the whipped cream in a 16-inch pastry bag fitted with a medium star tip and cover the chocolate completely with rosettes. Decorate the top and sides with candied violets. Serve chilled, cut into wedges. (The undecorated snowball may be refrigerated for a week or frozen for 6 months if wrapped airtight.)

Carolyn Buster's Chocolate Praline Mold

THE FIRST TIME **I tasted this dessert at "The Cottage" restaurant I was ecstatic. The combination of praline, chocolate, coffee, and rum blends together for an exceptional taste. This dessert can be molded to suit a holiday or special occasion theme.**

3 tablespoons sweet almond oil or flavorless vegetable oil
½ cup walnuts
12 ounces semisweet chocolate
½ cup sugar
¼ cup water
⅛ teaspoon cream of tartar
½ cup prepared strong coffee
¼ cup plus 2 teaspoons dark rum, divided
6 tablespoons unsalted butter at room temperature
2 cups whipping cream
2 tablespoons powdered sugar

Serves 8.

1. Place 1 tablespoon of the oil on a baking sheet and spread, using a paper towel. Set aside. Treat a 1¼-quart mold in the same way. Set aside.

2. Prep work: Coarsely chop the walnuts and set aside. Chop the chocolate and set aside. Combine sugar, water, and cream of tartar in a heavy skillet and bring to a boil over moderately high heat. Stir to dissolve the sugar and, using a pastry brush dipped in cold water, wash down any sugar crystals clinging to the sides of the skillet. Cook over high heat, rotating the skillet gently until the mixture is a light caramel color. Remove from heat and quickly add the nuts, rotating the skillet until the nuts are lightly coated and the caramel is golden brown. Be careful not to burn the caramel! Pour onto the oiled baking sheet. Cool until the mixture hardens. Break into pieces and pulverize the pieces a few at a time, in a food processor fitted with a steel blade. Set the praline powder aside.

3. In a heavy saucepan over low heat, melt the chocolate in the coffee and $\frac{1}{4}$ cup of the rum. Stir until smooth and add the butter and praline powder. Mix well and allow to cool slightly. Beat 1 cup of the whipping cream to stiff peaks and fold into the chocolate mixture. Pour into the prepared mold.

4. Chill, covered, at least 3 hours.

5. Run a flexible metal spatula around the inside of the mold. Carefully dip the outside of the mold into warm water. Invert a chilled serving plate over mold; invert with a sharp rap on the mold. Beat the remaining cream with the powdered sugar and remaining rum to stiff peaks. Spread over mold just before serving. (This mold can be frozen, provided it is properly wrapped, first in plastic wrap and then in aluminum foil.)

Carolyn Buster's Chocolate Praline Mold can be made in any 1¼ or 1½ quart mold you have available. Christmas and Easter molds are available, or make it in a simple rectangular terrine.

Vacherin Glacé au Chocolat

THE CRUNCHINESS OF THE meringue, the smoothness of the ice cream, and the richness of the sauce, create a delightful contrast in textures. You will enjoy making this dessert. It must be started a day in advance because the ice cream layer and the meringue layers both require the extra time.

1 quart chocolate ice cream
7 Grade A large egg whites at room temperature
1/4 teaspoon cream of tartar
1/4 teaspoon salt
1 3/4 cups sugar, divided
1 teaspoon pure vanilla
2 cups whipping cream
Chocolate Sauce (recipe follows)
Semisweet chocolate to grate on top

Serves 10–12.

1. Preheat oven to 200°F. Line 2 baking sheets with parchment paper. Using a 9-inch round cake pan as a guide, draw a circle in the center of each pan and set aside.

2. Prep work: Put the ice cream into a bowl and allow to soften slightly. Line the cake pan with plastic wrap, fill with the softened ice cream, and freeze overnight.

3. In a mixer bowl, beat the egg whites until foamy. Add the cream of tartar and salt and continue to beat. Add 1½ cups of the sugar, 2 tablespoons at a time. Beat well after each addition of sugar. Add the vanilla and beat to stiff peaks. This will take an additional 5–10 minutes. Spread the meringue equally on each 9-inch circle and smooth each with a small spatula.

4. Bake 2 hours. Turn off the oven and leave the layers in the oven to dry overnight.

5. Place one of the meringue layers on a serving plate; invert ice cream over meringue, removing pan and plastic wrap. Place remaining meringue layer over ice cream. Whip cream to soft peaks; add the remaining ¼ cup sugar and whip until stiff. Frost sides and top of cake with half of the whipped cream. Put remaining cream into a pastry bag fitted with a star tip and pipe rosettes around the outer edge of cake top. Spoon Chocolate Sauce inside rosette ring. Grate chocolate and sprinkle over the rosettes. (The cake can be frozen, finished, if you must, but the meringue layers tend to break down when frozen. To simplify preparation, bake the layers ahead and keep them in a tin in a cool, dark, dry place. They will stay crisp for a long while.)

Chocolate Sauce

1. Before you begin: Chop chocolates into small pieces and set aside.

2. Place sugar and 2 tablespoons of the cream in the top of a double boiler over boiling water. Stir to dissolve the sugar. Remove from the heat, leaving top of boiler over bottom, and add the chocolates. Stir until melted. Stir in the remaining cream and allow to cool.

½ ounce unsweetened chocolate

4 ounces semisweet chocolate

2 tablespoons sugar

¼ cup heavy cream, divided

While the recipe has its own Chocolate Sauce, different taste combinations may be had by using other chocolate sauces.

Carolyn Buster's Chocolate Rum Terrine

CAROLYN CREATED THIS dessert for her restaurant, "The Cottage." It was served to hundreds of people at a Northbrook, Illinois, chocolate festival and was highly acclaimed.

---

8 Grade A large eggs
8 ounces bittersweet
  chocolate (candy)
1 ounce chocolate coffee
  beans
1½ ounces prepared
  strong coffee
1 cup unsalted butter at
  room temperature
8 ounces sugar
3 ounces all-purpose flour
3 ounces dark rum
½ teaspoon salt
Chocolate Glaze (see
  index) or whipped
  cream

Serves 10–12.

1. Preheat oven to 350°F. Butter a 10-inch-by-3-inch-by-2½-inch terrine. Line the bottom with wax paper and butter the paper. Set aside. Set aside a pan large enough to hold the terrine as a water bath (bain marie).

2. Prep work: Separate the eggs and set the bowls aside. Fill a teapot with water, bring it to a boil, and keep hot. Chop the chocolate into small pieces and set aside.

3. In a heavy saucepan, melt the chocolate, chocolate coffee beans, and coffee. Stir until smooth. Remove from the heat and stir in the butter. Whisk until completely smooth. Beat yolks until light and fluffy, gradually adding sugar, flour, and rum. Stir egg yolk mixture into chocolate mixture and whisk until smooth. Beat whites until foamy, add salt, and continue beating until stiff, but not dry. Mix a third of the whites into the chocolate mixture, then carefully fold in the rest. Pour into the prepared terrine. Place terrine into the bain marie and fill the outside pan halfway up the sides with hot water.

4. Bake 1 hour and 15 minutes or until firm.

5. Allow terrine to cool to room temperature. Invert onto a serving plate. Peel off wax paper. Cover cake with a chocolate glaze (see index) or serve with softly whipped cream. Chill until ready to serve. (The terrine may be frozen before glazing, provided it is properly protected, first with plastic wrap and then with aluminum foil.)

Perla Meyers' Mousse au Chocolat Soufflé

THIS "MOUSSE SOUFFLÉ" is chocolaty and delicious—a magnificent combination of taste and texture. It comes from the first of Perla's three books, *The Seasonal Kitchen* (Holt, Rinehart and Winston). Guests will be enraptured with this dessert.

᠅

1. Preheat oven to 475°F. Butter the inside of a large 4-cup soufflé mold and sprinkle with sugar. Shake out the excess sugar.

2. Prep work: Separate the eggs and set 4 yolks and 6 whites aside. Chop the chocolate into small pieces and set aside.

3. In a mixer bowl, beat the yolks with ½ cup of sugar until the mixture is pale yellow. Stir in the rum and set aside. In a heavy saucepan melt the chocolate over very low heat. Beat in the butter 2 tablespoons at a time. Remove from heat and add the egg yolk mixture. In another bowl beat the whites until they form soft peaks but are not dry. Add a third of the egg white mixture to the chocolate mixture, then reverse the procedure, folding the chocolate mixture lightly into the remaining whites. It is best to use your hands. Do not worry if the egg whites are not entirely incorporated into the chocolate. Pour the mixture into the prepared soufflé mold.

4. Bake 12–15 minutes. The center should be a little runny.

5. Sprinkle the top with powdered sugar and serve immediately. A side bowl of ice cream can be served with the soufflé.

6. The soufflé cannot be frozen. If some soufflé is left over, serve it cold the next day with whipped cream. It will taste like a delicious chocolate brownie.

4 Grade A large egg yolks
6 Grade A large egg whites
6 ounces bittersweet chocolate
½ cup sugar
3 tablespoons rum
4 tablespoons unsalted butter at room temperature
Powdered sugar

Glossary

Bain Marie: A water bath. The larger outer vessel filled with hot water to insure even baking or cooking of the contents of a smaller, inner vessel.

Bake: To cook by dry oven heat.

Batter: A mixture of flour, liquid, and other ingredients that is thin enough to pour or drop from a spoon.

Beat: To mix by stirring briskly with a spoon, fork, whisk, or mixer.

Blend: To combine thoroughly so that the various ingredients cannot be distinguished.

Boil: To heat until vaporization, which can be determined by observing bubbling.

Caramelize: To heat sugar until it turns brown.

Chop: To cut into small pieces with a knife or blade.

Clarify: To make a liquid clear by separating suspended solids (as in separating solids in butter).

Coat a Spoon: A test for custards, etc., that leaves a thin film on a metal spoon.

Cream: To work one or more foods together into a smooth consistency.

Cut in: To mix edible fat into dry ingredients until texture is coarse and mealy.

Dash: To add a liquid ingredient in a very small amount (generally, less than a quarter teaspoonful).

Dough: A mixture of flour, liquid, and other ingredients worked into a soft mass.

Dust: To coat lightly with a dry ingredient.

Fold: To mix, using a light hand, in an over-and-over motion to lighten a substance with a heavier substance so no air or volume is lost.

Frost: To cover by spreading with a pastelike substance.

Frothy: Soft, light, and airy.

Garnish: To decorate by adding color or flavor.

Glaze: To cover with a thick, smooth and glossy coating.

Grate: To cut into small fine pieces.

Jellyroll Style: To roll up around a filling.

Knead: To mix by working with the hands and pressing the material being worked into itself.

Melt: To liquefy by heating.

Mix: To combine ingredients by stirring, beating, blending, or other method.

Mold: To form into a shape determined by the container.

Pinch: An amount of granular material that can be held between the thumb and forefinger (approximately ⅛ teaspoon).

Pipe: To trim by squeezing a soft substance through a pastry tube.

Purée: To mash or grind to a pastelike liquid consistency.

Ribbon: An egg yolk mixture mixed to the point where it falls off a beater blade in a thin sheet that looks like a ribbon.

Scald: To heat a liquid to a point just below its boiling point.

Sift: To create particles of uniform size by passing through a fine sieve.

Stiff but not dry: Egg whites beaten until they stand in stiff but moist and shiny peaks.

Stir: To move ingredients about to obtain uniformity in mixture or temperature.

Strain: To filter by passing through a screen or sieve.

Temper: To create uniformity in texture and appearance (with chocolate) through a procedure of heating and cooling to specific, closely defined temperature ranges.

Torte: To create additional thin layers by slicing through a cake layer on the horizontal.

Whip: To increase volume with the incorporation of air by beating with a whisk, beater, mixer, etc.

Zest: The hard, firm, colored part of citrus peel.

"T ASTE DEVELOPS
the production, the selection,
the preparation of everything
that can nourish us."

Brillat-Savarin

Sources

The following companies make catalogs available so you can have the luxury of shopping at home. They contain all the chocolate, chocolate supplies, and equipment you will need to work with this book.

Madame Chocolate
1940-C Lehigh Ave.
Glenview, IL 60025
(312) 720-3330

Chef's Catalog
3915 Commercial Ave.
Northbrook, IL 60062
(312) 480-9400

Kitchen Bazaar
4455 Connecticut Ave. N.W.
Washington, DC 20008
(202) 363-4600

Williams Sonoma
PO Box 7456
San Francisco, CA 94120
(415) 652-9007

Postscripts

Credits

How to Temper Chocolate (page 18), reprinted with permission from Elaine González, **Chocolate Artistry,** Contemporary Books, Inc., 1983. *Quotes from Billat-Savarin* (pages xi, 11, 23, 27, 31, and 201), from ***The Physiology of Taste,*** by Jean Anthelme Brillat-Savarin, translated by M. F. K. Fisher. *Jean Banchet's Gâteau au Chocolat* (page 46), reprinted with permission from Jean Banchet. *Doris Banchet's Italian Chocolate Torte* (page 64), reprinted with permission from Doris Banchet, 1984. *Bev Bennet's Brownies* (page 114), reprinted with permission from Bev Bennett, 1984. *Rose Levy Beranbaum's White Chocolate Frosting* (page 59), *Chocolate Truffle Torte* (page 62), *Sauce Hot Fudge Cordon Rose* (page 167); reprinted with permission from Rose Levy Beranbaum, Cordon Rose Cooking School, 1984. *Michael Bortz's Grand Marnier Truffles* (page 156), *Michael Bortz's Gianduja Bombe* (page 176); reprinted with permission from Michael Bortz, 1984. *Bête Noir* (page 80), reprinted with permission from Lora Brody, 1984. *"The Cottage" Chocolate Mousse Cake* (page 48), *Carolyn Buster's Chocolate Praline Mold* (page 192), *Carolyn Buster's Chocolate Rum Terrine* (page 196); reprinted with permission from Carolyn Buster, 1984. *Chocolate Marquise with Espresso Sauce* (page 54), reprinted with permission from the **Chicago Tribune,** 1984. *Dee Coutelle's Chewy, Gooey Chocolate Crêpes* (page 180), *Dee Coutelle's Chocolate Yeast Scones* (page 186); reprinted with permission from Dee Coutelle, 1984. *Baked Chocolate Rice Pudding* (page 41), *Million-Dollar Fudge* (page 158); reprinted with permission from Marion Cunningham, 1984. *Carol DeMasters' Pecan Brownies* (page 121), reprinted with permission from Carol DeMasters, 1984. *Jackie Etcheber's Banana Tart with Chocolate Sauce* (page 104), reprinted with permission from Jackie Etcheber, 1984. *Chocolate Raspberry Sandwich Cookies* (page 143), reprinted with permission from **The Food Enthusiast™,** P.O. Box 205, Birmingham, MI 48012. *Jane Salzfass Freiman's Chocolate Madeleines* (page 132), reprinted with permission from Jane Salzfass Freiman, **The Art of Food Processor Cooking,** Contemporary Books, Inc. *San Quentin Fudge Bars* (page 116), *Starlight Mint Surprise Cookies* (page 133); reprinted with permission of Ghirardelli Chocolate Company. Ghirardelli is a registered trademark of Golden Grain Macaroni Company and is used with the company's permission. *Elaine González's Torta Mexicana* (page 60), *Elaine González's Chocolate Truffles* (page 155), *Elaine González's Chocolate Sponge Roll* (page 178); reprinted with permission from Elaine González, **Chocolate Artistry,** Contemporary Books, Inc. *Barbara Grunes' Chocolate Flourless Cake* (page 74), *Chocolate Pound Cake* (page 81); reprinted with permission from Barbara Grunes, 1984. *Gianduja Cheesecake* (page 90), *Nancy Harris's Chocolate Sauce* (page 168); reprinted with permission from Nancy Harris, 1984. *Barbara Kafka's Chocolate Pôt de Crème* (page 34), *Barbara Kafka's Chocolate Sorbet* (page 188); reprinted with permission from Barbara Kafka, 1984. *Gianduja Cannoli* (page 106), reprinted with permission from Jane Lavine, 1984. *Abby Mandel's Boule de Neige* (page 190), reprinted with permission from Abby Mandel, 1984. *Alice Medrich's Chocolate Hazelnut Torte* (page 50), *Alice Medrich's Bûche au Chocolat Chantilly* (page 75); reprinted with permission from Alice Medrich, 1984. *Perla Meyers' Chocolate Mousse Roulade* (page 72), *Pearla Meyers' Chocolate Marquise with Pear Sauce* (page 68); reprinted with permission from Perla Meyers, 1984. *Perla Meyers' Mousse au Chocolat Soufflé* (page 197), reprinted with permission from Perla Meyers, **The Seasonal Kitchen,** Random House, Inc. *Café Cream Pie* (page 100), *Chocolate Swirl Coffeecake* (page 184), *Luscious Chocolate Almond Sauce* (page 171); reprinted with permission of The Nestlé Company, Inc., White Plains, New York. *Marble Cheesecake* (page 92), copyright © 1971 by The New York Times Company. Reprinted by permission. *Lutz Olkiewicz's Zurich Butter Truffles* (page 152), reprinted with permission from Lutz Olkiewicz, 1984. *Bob Paroubek's Fudge Mousse Cake with St. Cecelia Sauce* (page 78), reprinted with permission from Bob Paroubek, Toojay's, 1984. *Leslee Reis's Mocha Mousse* (page 37), *Leslee Reis's Caramel Trouffles* (page 154); reprinted with permission from Leslee Reis, 1984. *Susie Skoog's Chocolate Cherry Cake* (page 52), *Susie Skoog's Chocolate Whiskey Cake* (page 56), *Susie's Flourless Chocolate Layer Cake* (page 66), *Susie Skoog's Gianduja Cream Torte* (page 70), *Chocolate Fudge Cake à la Susie* (page 85), *Chocolate Almond Swirl Cheesecake* (page 94), *Susie Skoog's Valrhôna Orange Pie* (page 99), *Susie Skoog's Chocolate-Caramel Brownies* (page 112), *Skooger Doodles* (page 139), *Monster Cookies* (page 146), *Susie Skoog's White Chocolate Apricot Sauce* (page 169); reprinted with permission from Susie Skoog, 1984. *Gabino Sotelino's White Chocolate Mousse* (page 36), reprinted with permission from Gabino Sotelino, 1984. *Barbara Tuleja's Terrine of Bittersweet Chocolate with Fruits and Nuts* (page 174), reprinted with permission from Barbara Tuleja, 1984. *Albicocca Cioccolato* (Chocolate Apricot Gelato) (page 189), reprinted with permission from Al Gelato, Mike Winter, 1984. *Jolene Worthington's Chocolate Velvet Cheesecake* (page 88), *Jolene Worthington's Chocolate Pie Crust* (page 103), *Shiny Brownie Glaze* (page 125); reprinted with permission from Jolene Worthington, 1984.

Index